LET'S FIX MEDICARE,
REPLACE MEDICAID,
AND REPEAL THE AFFORDABLE CARE ACT

LET'S FIX MEDICARE, REPLACE MEDICAID,

AND REPEALTHE AFFORDABLE CARE ACT

HERE IS WHY AND HOW.

LINDSAY L. PRATT, M.D.

202 S. Pebble Beach Blvd.
Sun City Center, Florida 33573
813 394 5132
LPratt2269@AOL.com

authorHOUSE®

AuthorHouse™
1663 Liberty Drive
Bloomington, IN 47403
www.authorhouse.com
Phone: 1-800-839-8640

First published by AuthorHouse   01/06/2012

ISBN: 978-1-4678-8237-8 (sc)
ISBN: 978-1-4678-8238-5 (ebk)

Printed in the United States of America

Any people depicted in stock imagery provided by Thinkstock are models, and such images are being used for illustrative purposes only.
Certain stock imagery © Thinkstock.

This book is printed on acid-free paper.

Index

Prologue

If you are you a Medicaid patient, or if you are a patient without any health insurance, I'm aware of the difficulty you have had, and are having, obtaining your healthcare services, and I agree with you. The existing investor owned and profit driven healthcare delivery system is not a friendly delivery system for those patients unable to pay for their healthcare services. But, in its place, if you are supporting the Affordable Care Act, please reconsider your support, and consider the recommendations in this book.

In this book, I'm offering everyone without the ability to pay for their healthcare services, the opportunity to obtain the same quality, comprehensive, and easily available healthcare services as the services provided patients who are purchasing their healthcare services. Neither Medicaid nor the Affordable Care Act can provide those same services, and the reasons why are discussed in this book.

Furthermore, in addition to the difficulty patients with Medicaid and without health insurance are having obtaining their healthcare services, patients with health insurance, regardless of its source, need to be prepared for the probability, not the possibility, of their having difficulty obtaining their healthcare services in two years when the Affordable Care Act becomes their healthcare delivery system.

The frustration with Medicaid's inadequate services is understandable, and the confusion about the future among patients with health insurance is understandable. The problem for both is the many articles written about what is happening, and will be happening, in healthcare have not correctly identified the causes of, or offered realistic solutions for, what is happening, and will be happening, in healthcare. The problem with those article's is their misinformation and their use of conjecture. Misinformation is offered in some of those articles to support the author's agenda.

Conjecture is used by other authors. They are too young to have witnessed what happened during the 1950s and 1960s to cause what has happened in healthcare.

As a practicing physician/surgeon during the 1950s and 1960s, I witnessed what happened during those years to cause our healthcare delivery system's present problems. Also, having witnessed the cause, I'm aware fixing Medicare, replacing Medicaid, and repealing the Affordable Care Act are realistic solutions for all of healthcare's present problems. Defending those three solutions is the message in this book

Forward

Congress has foolishly and irresponsibly proposed and adopted the Affordable Care Act as the solution for what is happening in healthcare. But instead of providing the solution, the Act is making what is happening worse. The Affordable Care Act must be repealed.

It is an aberration. It is not a healthcare document. The Act was never intended to provide patients quality, comprehensiveness, and easily available healthcare services less expensively.

How could it? The Act was written by bureaucrats who do not practice medicine, and who do not possess the knowledge necessary to know what is necessary to provide patients quality, comprehensive, and easily available healthcare services less expensively.

Instead, of being a healthcare document, the Affordable Care Act is a political document. The Act was conceived to offer government the opportunity it has been seeking since the 1950s to control healthcare. Controlling healthcare creates an enormous voting block dependent on government for their healthcare services. Such a voting block provides politicians enormous political power. More about this is discussed in the book.

But, let's put aside the fact the legislation is a self serving political document. A more serious problem for the public to consider is the Act gives government the administrative responsibility of managing our country's future healthcare delivery system. Is our government capable of managing and funding a system that provides more than three hundred million people their healthcare services?

Let's examine some facts. Social Security needs to be maintained.

But, although trillions of dollars have been paid into the Social Security "Trust" Fund over the years, its future solvency is in question. Why? The government has mismanaged the fund.

Reports have confirmed Congress has spent many of the dollars paid into the Social Security "Trust" Fund to fund other social programs, and Congress has replaced those dollars with IOUs. IOUs to be paid by tax payers. For example, the funds for Social Security have been reduced by more than one hundred billion dollars during 2011. An election year political program to attract voters has been introduced reducing the pay roll contributions ["tax"] to Social Security by three or four percentage points. The political rhetoric is the program is a tax reduction. Nonsense! Now, they want to extend the program for another year and cause the Social Security Fund to lose another more than one hundred billion dollars.

The Transportation Dept. is another example of government mismanagement. The Dept. has received trillions of dollars over the years from gasoline taxes, etc. But in 2011, the Dept. has fiscal problems, and has the need to borrow money to maintain our highway's infrastructure. Why? Government has mismanaged the fund. Congress has spent many of the tax dollars collected to fund our highway's infrastructure to fund other social programs.

The Department of Education is another example of government mismanagement. The Dept. has received trillions of dollars over many years, and each year the Dept. wants more dollars. But the Dept. has failed to provide our country an education system as good as, or as inexpensive as, the education systems in most other industrialized countries. Why? The government has allowed increasing amounts of education's tax dollars fund a hugh, expensive, and unnecessary education bureaucracy for political expediency.

Education's decisions should be returned to local communities were those decisions were made when I was attending the public school system in the 1930s.

Also, think about this. If you think the influence of lobbyists is a problem, and if you think the "legislative favors" politicians offer to obtain political contributions are a problem, just wait until government is controlling a system as large as healthcare.

Need I go on?

The historical evidence supports the obvious. Our government is incapable of administering large bureaucracies like the one required to fund and to provide EVERYONE [more than three hundred million people] their necessary healthcare services.

The public should have their representatives in Congress repeal the Affordable Care Act. As an alternative, the public should consider supporting the recommendations in this book.

Why is the book's proposal to fix Medicare and replace Medicaid better than the Affordable Care Act? The following are several reasons, and they, plus others, are discussed in the book. First is the probability the Affordable Care Act's health insurance will be worthless within a decade. Health insurance can only purchase healthcare's services. It cannot provide those services. Physicians are necessary to provide those services, and the Act has not provided the career incentives necessary to attract the BEST OF OUR YOUTH to become our country's future physicians. In contrast, the proposals to fix Medicare and replace Medicaid will provide the career incentives necessary to attract the best of our youth to become our future physicians.

Second, the name Affordable Care Act is an oxymoron. The Act is not "affordable". Instead, it will increase the cost of healthcare's services, and it will make those services more difficult to obtain. In contrast, the proposal to fix Medicare will restore fiscal sanity to our healthcare delivery system [provide the necessary reductions in healthcare's costs] and enable everyone to continue to receive their necessary healthcare services.

Third, from a demographic prospective, the Affordable Care Act will not be able to fund the healthcare needs of our increasing senior population. 80% of healthcare's costs are created by only 20% of the population, and seniors are most of the 20%. Our population will be increasing, but the increase will not be caused by an increasing number of births. Instead, the increase will be caused to a declining mortality rate. People are living longer, and the senior population is projected to increase by 50% in the next decade. Since the Affordable Care Act has neither addressed, nor reduced, any of the causes of healthcare's increasing costs, the Act will not be able to fund the healthcare needs of our increasing senior population without rationing.

Fourth, in contrast to the Affordable Care Act, the proposal to fix Medicare offers seniors, the largest users of healthcare's services, the opportunity to continue to receive ALL of their necessary healthcare services.

Five, the Affordable Care Act is a political document. In contrast, this book is a healthcare document. The book recommends five changes in the existing private healthcare delivery that will reduce healthcare's costs by at least 40%, and will have healthcare's costs become affordable once again. In addition, the book proposes the replacement of Medicaid with free healthcare facilities.

This book's recommendations and proposals are going to anger many individuals and organizations who have acquired power and profits by their misuse of health insurance. But the book was not written to please. It was written to inform the public about how their obsession with health insurance is allowing politicians and business entrepreneurs, along with their investors, to change our previously patient driven and not-for-profit healthcare delivery system into a bureaucratically administered and profit driven business system.

I hope you enjoy reading what you have probably never heard about, thought about, or considered important.

Introduction

The Time Has Come

The time has come to challenge the public's acquired sense of entitlement for, and their debilitating dependency on, the many social programs introduced during the past several decades. The cost of those programs is bankrupting our country. Medicare, Medicaid, and the health insurance provided by employers have become three of those entitlements. But, not one of the three is an entitlement, and the possession of health insurance, regardless of its source, must never be considered necessary to obtain healthcare's services.

Furthermore, the time has come to acknowledge that everyone has the right to obtain their necessary healthcare services. Yes, everyone has the right to obtain the same quality, comprehensive, and easily available healthcare services. However, health insurance is not the answer for providing everyone that right. For example, over the past fifty years, the possession of Medicaid has not offered everyone without the ability to pay for their healthcare services the same opportunity to obtain their healthcare services.

Instead of health insurance, the best way to provide everyone the opportunity to obtain their necessary healthcare services is to restore the healthcare delivery system that existed prior to 1960s.

Few, if any, patients in 2011, or their healthcare providers, are aware of the benefits our country's healthcare delivery system provided every patient prior to the 1960s. At the time, the patient's dollars were purchasing healthcare's services, and healthcare's services were affordable. Those affordable services provided affordable health insurance programs most individuals and some employers were able to purchase. Patients unable to purchase their healthcare services were able to obtain quality, comprehensive, and easily available healthcare services in the free healthcare facilities [discussed in Chapter Eleven]. With few, if any, exceptions, everyone had the opportunity to obtain the same quality, comprehensive, and easily available healthcare services prior to the 1960s.

But after the 1960s, unregulated "insurance" dollars were replacing the patient's dollars as the primary source of payment for healthcare's services. Those "insurance" dollars were changing a previously patient driven private healthcare delivery system into an investor owned and profit driven business system. What followed was a service availability problem and a cost problem.

The service availability problem was created by the closure of the free healthcare facilities. In the late 1960s, the passage of Medicare and Medicaid had offered an increasing number of patients health insurance, and fewer patients were seeking free healthcare services. Those free healthcare facilities began to close, and by the early 1970s, all of those free facilities had closed. The absence of those free facilities had made obtaining healthcare's services increasingly difficult for some patients with Medicare, for many patients with Medicaid, and for all patients without the ability to pay for their healthcare services. All of those patients had to obtain their services from private practitioners, and increasing numbers of private practitioners were no longer offering free healthcare services or willing to accept the reduced insurance reimbursements offered by Medicare and Medicaid.

The cost problem after the 1960s was caused by the failure of the employers and the tax payer's [government] supplying those "insurance" dollars to monitor either what those dollars were purchasing or the increasing charges for what those dollars were purchasing. Also, there were many special interests entering healthcare after the 1950s seeking, and obtaining, some of those "insurance" dollars unchallenged.

A fact: Prior to the 1960s, more patients had the opportunity to receive better quality, more comprehensive, more available, and less expensive healthcare services than they were able to receive after the 1960s.

Have we not learned from the past? Instead of health insurance, more patients will benefit by restoring a healthcare delivery system similar to the one that existed prior to the 1960s.

One final comment about health insurance. Few individuals understand the limitations of health insurance. To repeat: Health insurance can ONLY purchase healthcare's service. It cannot provide healthcare's services. Only physicians, and other healthcare providers, can provide healthcare's services. Therefore, without physicians, and the other healthcare providers, health insurance is worthless.

In addition to acknowledging the right of everyone to obtain their necessary healthcare's services, the time has come to acknowledge profiting from an individual's need for those services is unacceptable. Why? Healthcare is not part of the free market economy. In a free market economy, an individual has the option of deciding whether or not they want to obtain a service or a product, and the individual has the option of deciding the price they are willing to pay for the service or product. Accordingly, those providing the service or product have the right to decide the price of their service or product, and they have the right to obtain a profit from the sale of their service or product.

However, healthcare is different. A patient has not had the option of deciding whether or not they wanted to acquire their illness or their disability, and they have not had the option of deciding what they are willing to pay to treat their illness or their disability. They have acquired the illness or disability, and they must pay whatever is necessary to treat their illness or disability. Therefore, those providing the treatment do not have the right to charge whatever "the market will pay" for their treatment or the right to profit from providing the treatment.

Applying price controls to healthcare's services is appropriate. [The Provider Reimbursement Formula discussed in Chapter Seven]. Furthermore, since health insurance will remain one of the options the public will have to obtain their healthcare services, the insurance companies offering health insurance need to be, and can function effectively as, not-for-profit companies.

Entrepreneurs and investors seeking profits are welcome and encouraged to participate in our free market economy, but they do not belong in the healthcare.

Chapter One

Healthcare's Increasing Costs

Healthcare's costs began to increase during the 1960s, and why those costs increased is similar to why the cost of our country's manufactured products increased. Healthcare's costs began to increase because of the many costly demands made on the employer's, and later the tax payer's "insurance" dollars. The cost of our country's manufactured products began to increase during the1960s because of the many costly demands made on the employer's dollars.

Prior to the 1960s, most of the dollars purchasing Healthcare's services were dollars supplied by patients, and patients were using their dollars responsibly to purchase their Healthcare's services. The only demand made on those patient's dollars was to pay the cost of the services patients were receiving. Therefore, prior to the 1960s, one patient dollar was able to purchase one unit of Healthcare's services, and the cost of Healthcare's services was stable.

But, during the 1960s, Healthcare's costs were increasing. The problem was the patient's dollars purchasing Healthcare's services were being replaced with "insurance" dollars supplied by employers and later by tax payers [Medicare and Medicaid]. Patients began to use those "insurance" dollars irresponsibly. Patients were purchasing medically unnecessary healthcare services, and they were indifferent to the increasing cost of those services. In addition to the patient's irresponsible use of those "insurance" dollars, additional costly demands were being made on those "insurance" dollars by other special interests during the 1960s and1970s. [Discussed in Chapter Three]. Those many costly demands on the employer's and tax payer's "insurance" dollars were requiring more of those "insurance" dollars be provided to pay those costs, and those additional dollars were increasing healthcare's costs.

Initially, neither the employers nor the government [tax payers] supplying those "insurance" dollars were concerned with how many of their "insurance" dollars were being used to pay those costly demands. But by the late 1960s, Healthcare's costs were increasing more rapidly than the rate of inflation, and many more of those "insurance" dollars were required to purchase the same unit of Healthcare's services only one of the patient's dollars had purchased previously. The need for those additional "insurance" dollars had increased Healthcare's costs, and those increasing costs were soon to become unsustainable.

The reason why the costs of our manufactured products were increasing during the same time our healthcare costs were increasing is similar. Prior to the 1960s, while patients were using their dollars to purchase their healthcare services, employees were using their dollars to purchase their healthcare services and to save and invest for their retirement. The cost of our country's manufactured products was stable. But during the 1950s, and especially during the 1960s, the employee's dollars that had been purchasing their healthcare services and being saved for their retirement were being replaced with dollars supplied by their employers. In addition to employees demanding their employers increase their salaries, employees were making additional demands on their employer's dollars. The employer's were having to provide their employees their health insurance, later a retirement income, and later health insurance after their retirement. Recovering those costly demands required employers to increase the cost of their manufactured products.

Initially, employers paying those costly employee benefits were not concerned with the cost of those benefits or the increasing cost of their manufactured products. But as the employee's demands for more increased, recovering the cost of those demands required the cost of the employer's manufactured products to increase and soon those increasing costs become unsustainable.

Attempts have been made to claim Healthcare's increasing costs were caused by the cost of new technologies and not by the irresponsible and costly demands made on the "insurance" dollars. Although those technologies have added to Healthcare's increasing costs, the major cause of Healthcare's increasing costs has been, and continues to be, the many unchallenged and irresponsible costly demands made on the employer's and the tax payer's "insurance" dollars.

One example, among many, of an irresponsible and costly demand made on the employer's and tax payer's "insurance" dollars was one of my experiences as the Medical Director of an HMO. The HMO was able to obtain MRIs for $600. However, the same MRI was costing a private patient $1,000. There are other examples of the HMO's smaller payments for the same Healthcare's services private patients were purchasing.

Over several decades, paying the increasing costs of the demands made on the employer's and the tax payer's "insurance" dollars have made the cost of Healthcare's services in 2011 to become unaffordable and no longer sustainable.

Before discussing some of those irresponsible and costly demands made on the employer's and the tax payer's "insurance" dollars, two of those demands, Medicare and Medicaid, need be discussed separately.

Chapter Two

Medicare and Medicaid

Medicare and Medicaid have become two of the public's acquired health insurance "entitlements", and both have contributed significantly to Healthcare's increasing costs. Most of the patients who create 80% of Healthcare's costs are Medicare patients.

Why did the introduction of Medicare and Medicaid contribute to increasing Healthcare's costs? Prior to Medicare, many Medicare patients had been purchasing one of the affordable health insurance programs, and other Medicare patients had been receiving their healthcare services in the free healthcare facilities. But after the introduction of Medicare, tax payer's began to provide the "insurance" dollars necessary to pay the cost of the healthcare services Medicare patients were receiving. Medicaid created a similar cost problem. Most Medicaid patients had been receiving their healthcare services in free healthcare facilities, but after Medicaid was introduced, tax payer's "insurance" dollars began to pay for their services.

In addition to tax payers having to pay the cost of Medicare's and Medicaid's healthcare services, tax payers were having to pay the additional cost of the "political favors" politicians were offering Medicare's and Medicaid's suppliers and users.

The need for tax payer's to pay for Medicare's and Medicaid's healthcare services and to pay for the politician's "political favors" required "insurance" dollars be provided that had not been required previously in healthcare, and those additional tax payer's "insurance" dollars were contributing to Healthcare's increasing costs.

Many individuals, with whom I have discussed the issue, believe Medicare and Medicaid were introduced to benefit the public.

Wrong! Those individuals have been misguided by the misinformation offered in the political rhetoric and print media by a government whose credibility is becoming increasing questionable. Instead of being introduced to benefit patients, the evidence supports that Congress introduced Medicare and Medicaid to destroy the private healthcare delivery system and advance government's opportunity to control healthcare. No, this is not paranoia, and here's the evidence I have witnessed.

In the early 1950s when I began treating patients, there were members in Congress seeking to obtain legislation creating a National Health Service similar to England's. But, most of the public was satisfied with the private healthcare delivery system. There was no public support for a National Health Service.

How was the public's support for a National Health Service to be obtained?

Fortunately for those Congresspersons, the introduction of the employer's health insurance programs during the 1950s was creating a sense of health insurance entitlement among a large segment of the population. By the 1960s, the public's sense of health insurance entitlement had provided Congress the opportunity to offer those patients receiving their healthcare services in the free healthcare facilities the opportunity to obtain "free" health insurance.

Again, those Congresspersons were fortunate. Three healthcare issues had surfaced during the 1950s that were favorable to the public's acceptance of the government's "free" health insurance in the 1960s.

One issue was the entitlement culture. If employers were providing their employees health insurance, why wasn't the government entitled to offer everyone else health insurance? The second issue was Healthcare's increasing costs. The costly demands being made on the employer's "insurance" dollars by an increasing number of special interests during the 1950s and into the 1960s were increasing the cost of Healthcare's services. Those increasing costs were causing concerns among many individuals about their ability to continue to purchase their previously affordable Healthcare's services. The third issue was the support from an increasing number of Healthcare's providers and suppliers. The more people with insurance, the more profits for them.

With an awareness of these three issues, and a supporting media, Congress began a marketing program in the early 1960s. Congress was aware the increasing number of individuals with their employer's insurance would not be interested in receiving the government's "free" health insurance. But the large number of patients in the free healthcare facilities and retired seniors with limited incomes would be interested. Government began a marketing program that vilified the services offered in the existing free healthcare facilities, and patients in those free facilities were told they could do better with, and should have the opportunity to obtain, health insurance. Many seniors, along with the indigent, "bought" the political rhetoric and supported the legislation creating Medicare and Medicaid in the mid 1960s.

Although a large segment of the population was now dependent on government for their healthcare services, neither Medicare nor Medicaid had replaced the public's support for the private healthcare delivery system. Instead, Medicare and Medicaid had provided more patients the insurance necessary for their participation in the private healthcare delivery system.

It became obvious to those in Congress seeking a National Health Service the public's support for the private healthcare delivery system had to be destroyed. But how? The answer was provided in the 1970s.

Again those Congresspersons seeking a National Health Service were fortunate. During the decades of the 1950s and 1960s, the billions of employer's and tax payer's "insurance" dollars flowing into the healthcare delivery system were attracting business entrepreneurs. Those entrepreneurs wanted some of those dollars. But they had no way of entering healthcare. To enter healthcare, they began to lobby Congress to create legislation offering them the opportunity to enter the healthcare delivery system.

Those entrepreneurs were fortunate. Those members in Congress seeking to destroy the public's support for the private healthcare delivery system were aware Medicare and Medicaid had not increased the public's sense of dependency on government. Medicare and Medicaid had provided patients in the free healthcare facilities health insurance, but what was needed was an alternative healthcare insurer that could attract patients away from the existing private health insurance industry. If enough of the private health insurance industry's patients became policyholders in an alternative healthcare insurer, those patients would become dependent on the policies of the alternative healthcare insurer. Their dependency on the alternative insurer's policies would destroy the private healthcare delivery system.

The creation of Medicare and Medicaid had not created the alternative insurer Congress had been seeking, and neither had destroyed the public's support for, or desire to participation in, the private healthcare delivery system. However, those business entrepreneurs offered Congress its opportunity to establish the alternative healthcare insurer it had been seeking.

Congress recruited those business entrepreneurs, and together they created the managed healthcare industry legislation in the1970s. The legislation provided the entrepreneurs their opportunity to enter healthcare, and after entering healthcare, they recruited investors. Together with their investors, those entrepreneurs established the investor owned and profit driven HMOs and multi-hospital management companies. The HMOs became the alternative healthcare insurers Congress had been seeking. Over a decade, those HMOs had enroll enough of the private health insurance industry's policyholders to collapse the private healthcare delivery system. How was this accomplished?

The business entrepreneurs in the HMO industry were aware80% of the public required infrequent healthcare services and created less than 20% of Healthcare's costs. Accordingly, HMOs enrolled only "healthy" individuals initially. I was employed for a short period of time as the Medical Director of an HMO following my retirement. One of my responsibilities was to review the medical records of those individuals seeking to become enrollees in the HMO. If any of those individuals had medical problems, they would be denied enrollment in the HMO.

Enrolling only "healthy" individuals offered the HMO industry the opportunity to offer less expensive premiums than the premiums offered by the existing private health insurance industry. The private insurance industry had more expensive premiums because the industry was providing its policyholders with existing medical problems their more expensive healthcare services.

The HMO's less expensive premiums were attracting many of the private health insurance industry's "healthy" policyholders, and by the 1980s, the loss of those "healthy" policyholder's premiums was causing the cost of the private health insurance industry's premiums to become more expensive. The industry had to continue to pay the cost of the more expensive services required by its policyholders with medical problems without the help of their "healthy" policyholder's premiums. Attempts to control their costs required the private health insurance industry to refuse new policyholders with existing medical problems. But as more of their "healthy" policyholders enrolled in HMOs, the cost of the private health insurance industry's premiums were no longer competitive. By the 1990s, the HMO industry had replaced the private health insurance industry as a major healthcare insurer.

The loss of the private health insurance industry was followed by the collapse of the private healthcare delivery system. Those individuals enrolling in the HMOs no longer had the freedom to select the healthcare services and providers of their choice. Instead, those HMO enrollees were required to accept their HMO's providers and their HMO's other services and policies. The HMOs had provided those Congresspersons seeking a National Health Service the opportunity to destroy the private healthcare delivery system. Also, the increasing number of those

Congresspersons seeking a National Health Service in both houses in Congress, enabled them to pass the Affordable Care Act legislation, and the legislation provided Congress the control of the healthcare delivery system in the United States it had been seeking since the 1950s. Their control would offer them the enormous political power they had been seeking. The Affordable Care Act in two years would create a large voting block dependent on government for their healthcare services.

Government's control of healthcare raises two questions the public needs to ponder. First, is the loss of the private healthcare delivery system a threat to the quality, the comprehensiveness, and the availability of our country's future healthcare services? If you are a senior, you best give this question serious consideration. Second, is the government capable of managing and funding a system as large as the healthcare delivery system in the United States? Everyone needs to give this question serious consideration.

Wake up America! The answers to both questions should be obvious.

Neither Medicare, Medicaid, the Affordable Care Act, nor the investor owned and profit driven manage healthcare industry were created by Congress to benefit the public. Instead, Medicare and Medicaid were created to destroy what the public is about to learn was their best healthcare friend—the private healthcare delivery system. The manage healthcare industry was created to provide the alternative healthcare insurer necessary to successfully compete with, and ultimately destroy, the public's two best friends—the private health insurance industry and the private healthcare delivery system. The Affordable Care Act was created to obtain a large voting block dependent on government for their healthcare services.

Isn't it obvious? Or is the public unaware of the dangers inherent in the roles both Congress and the managed healthcare industry are assuming in healthcare. A poorly informed public, along with their acquired sense of health insurance entitlement, has many individuals believing government's and the managed healthcare industry's control of healthcare is not a threat. Wrong! Although both are providing, and paying for, the health insurance most of the public is receiving, the public

9

has not considered the consequences of having received that insurance. All of the decisions about their future healthcare services are going to be made by government bureaucrats and by the business entrepreneurs and their investors in the managed healthcare industry. What a price to pay for health insurance that will probably be worthless within a decade. Yes, the probability of a physician shortage within a decade is real, and the probability that many of those who become physicians will not have come from the best of our youth is real. Yes, you will have your insurance, but what good is that insurance when you have fewer, and less qualified, physicians providing your healthcare services.

Let's take a closer look at why government's control of healthcare [the Affordable Care Act] has made the public the loser. The Affordable Care Act offers the public questionable, if any, benefits. First, the legislation will not reduce Healthcare's costs. It has not addressed any of the many costly demands made on the healthcare dollar that have reduced the dollar's purchasing power and increased Healthcare's costs. Without addressing those costs, reducing Healthcare's costs is not possible—unless the legislation plans to ration Healthcare's services. Is rationing in the Affordable Care Act's future? Of course it is. Again, is it not obvious!

80% of Healthcare's costs are created by only 20% of the population, and the Affordable Care Act has not challenged, or reduced, any of the costly demands that have caused 20% of the public to create 80% of Healthcare's costs. Accordingly, to reduce healthcare's costs, the Act will have to ration the services offered to the 20% who create 80% of Healthcare's costs. Unfortunately, seniors comprise most of the 20%, and the number of seniors is projected to increase by about 50% in the next decade. Too bad seniors!

Don't be fooled. If you are a senior, the Affordable Care Act will be rationing your healthcare services.

The politicians sponsoring the Affordable Care Act are aware the Act will require rationing senior's Healthcare's services. But rationing those services does not create a problem for those politicians. The

Act is a win-win for them. First, since about 80% of our population require infrequent healthcare services, politicians know the majority of our population will be satisfied with the services offered by the Affordable Care Act. Second, since those 80% create only about 20% of Healthcare's costs, politicians will be able say the Act has reduced Healthcare's costs.

Another reason the Affordable Care Act will not be able to reduce Healthcare's costs is the cost of the enormous bureaucracy required to administer the legislation.

When I hear the comments of many individuals about the "success" of socialized medicine programs in other countries, I'm aware those comments come from individuals who have not considered the differences between the United States and those countries with socialized healthcare programs. First, most of those countries are smaller than either the states of California or Texas. The size of the bureaucracies required to administer their socialized medicine programs cannot be compared to the huge bureaucracy required to administer the Affordable Care Act in the United States. Second, while there are countries as large as the United States, like Australia and Canada, those countries do not have the same population density as does the United States. For example, Australia's population is less that 35 million while the population in the United States is more than three hundred million. The bureaucracies required to manage the funding of, and the delivery of, Healthcare's services to a population of more than three hundred million in the United States will be administratively cumbersome, inefficient, and enormously expensive.

In addition to the Affordable Care Act not being able to reduce Healthcare's costs, the legislation will not be able to either maintain the quality of our country's healthcare services or the availability of those services. The Affordable Care Act can only OFFER Healthcare's services. It cannot PROVIDE those services. Physicians and other healthcare providers are necessary to PROVIDE the Affordable Care Act's services. Also, the quality of those services will depend on the abilities of the physicians, and the other healthcare providers, providing those services. Will the best of our youth question becoming a physician whose career opportunities and compensation depend on the unpredictable whims of another politically appointed government bureaucracy? And, will many who become physicians not come from the best of our youth? The future quality of the Affordable Care Act's healthcare services has to be questioned as well as the availability of its services. Don't doubt me! The probability of a physician shortage within a decade is real.

Another question raised by the passage of the Affordable Care Act is whether or not our Republic will survive? Has the ability of the executive and the legislative branches of government to adopt laws without considering any opposition from the public introduced tyranny? Also, has the constitutional separation of the executive and legislative branches of government become blurred? What about the judicial branch of our government? So far, the responses to the Affordable Care Act's legal challenges appear to suggest the judicial branch of our government has become politicized. Judges appear to be making decisions based on their political ideology rather than on the constitution.

Returning to Medicare and Medicaid, Medicare needs to be preserved. It will provide seniors better healthcare services less expensively than the Affordable Care Act can provide them. Fixing Medicare is possible, and it will provide the affordable health insurance Medicare, employers, and other individuals can afford to purchase. The proposals to fix Medicare in this book will provide at least a 40% reduction in Healthcare's costs. Also, fixing Medicare will preserve a fee-for-service private healthcare delivery system which is a delivery system providing the career incentives necessary to attract the best of our youth to continue to become our future physicians and other healthcare providers.

Furthermore, replacing Medicaid with the free healthcare facilities proposed in this book [Chapter Eleven] is the best way to provide more patients better healthcare services less expensively than either Medicaid or the Affordable Care Act's proposed changes in Medicaid can provide.

Chapter Three

Those Costly Demands That Have Increased Healthcare's Costs

P rior to the 1960s, patients supplying the dollars purchasing Healthcare's services did not allow costly demands to be made on their dollars. The only demand made on those dollars was to pay the patient's providers, and one patient dollar was able to purchase one unit of Healthcare's services.

However, after the 1960s, most of the dollars purchasing healthcare's services were "insurance" dollars supplied by employer's and tax payer's, and many costly demands were being made on those "insurance" dollars that had never been allowed to be made on the patient's dollars. Paying the cost of those demands required employer's and tax payer's provide more of their "insurance "dollars to purchase the same unit of Healthcare's services only one of the patient's dollars had purchased previously. The need for those additional employer's and tax payer's "insurance" dollars was increasing Healthcare's costs.

Perhaps the initial demand made on the employer's and tax payer's "insurance" dollars was the need to pay the operating expenses of the health insurance industry. Employers were engaging health insurance companies to distribute their dollars to their employee's healthcare providers. Those companies had management, investor, administrative, and other operating expenses. Paying the cost of those insurance company's expenses required employers provide more of their dollars than the dollars required previously to purchase only Healthcare's services for their employees. The need for those additional dollars was reducing their purchasing power and increasing the employer's cost of providing their employees their healthcare services.

In addition to the additional employer's dollars required to pay the expenses of the health insurance industry, employers found themselves having to provide more dollars to pay the cost of their employees increasing utilization of medically unnecessary healthcare services, and the increasing provider charges for those services. The need for those additional employer's "insurance" dollars was further reducing their purchasing power and adding to the employer's cost of providing their employee's their healthcare services.

During the 1960s, both Medicare and Medicaid were introduced, and paying the cost of the healthcare services for Medicare's and Medicaid's patients required tax payers provide "insurance" dollars that had not been needed in healthcare previously. Prior to Medicare and Medicaid, many Medicare patients, and all Medicaid patients, had been receiving their healthcare services in free healthcare facilities. But after Medicare and Medicaid were introduced, tax payers were providing the "insurance" dollars required to purchase their healthcare services. The need for those tax payer's "insurance" dollars was increasing Healthcare's costs and reducing the purchasing power of Healthcare's "insurance" dollars.

In addition to having to supply the dollars necessary to purchase Medicare's and Medicaid's healthcare services, tax payers were supplying additional dollars to pay for the "political favors" both Medicare and Medicaid were offering their suppliers and users. An example of those "political favors" is the need to purchase new wheelchairs, electric scooters, prosthetic arms and legs, and other expensive healthcare items for Medicare and Medicaid patients. Instead, of purchasing new items, those items should be returned to be used by other Medicare and Medicaid patients when the patients using them no longer need them.

However, when patients no longer require the use of those items, neither MEDICARE NOR MEDICAID WANTS THEM RETURNED. If those items were returned, other Medicare and Medicaid patients in need of those items could use them rather than Medicare and Medicaid purchasing new items for those patients.

In addition to Medicare not wanting those expensive items returned, most social service agencies and nursing homes do not want those items either. Those agencies are inundated with many of those items donated by Medicare and Medicaid patients. Also, local consignment stores do not want those items. They have no resale value. The problem? Medicare and Medicaid will purchase new items for patients. Therefore, those "used" healthcare items have no market value.

Medicare and Medicaid could save hundreds of millions of tax payer's "insurance" dollars each year if the expensive items they have purchased were returned after the individual using them no longer needs them. However, a question for the public to ponder. Will the contributions to politicians for their political campaigns from the lobbyists representing the manufacturers of these expensive items allow Congress to have those items returned to Medicare and Medicaid? Of course not, and this is why an informed public should not want government in healthcare.

Wake up America! Yes, government is providing you Medicare and Medicaid, but you are paying unnecessary taxes to support Medicare's and Medicaid's irresponsible purchasing practices. Get government out of healthcare.

Another costly demand made on the employer's and tax payer's "insurance" dollars was the need to use many of those dollars to defend healthcare lawsuits. During the 1950s, and into the 1960s, billions of unregulated employer and tax payer "insurance" dollars were flowing into the healthcare delivery system, and those dollars were attracting attorneys. They wanted some of those dollars, and to obtain them, attorneys began to increase the number of malpractice lawsuits. By the 1980s, an estimated 50 billion of those "insurance" dollars were required each year to pay the cost of engaging the attorneys required to defend Healthcare's many lawsuits. The need for those billions of "insurance" dollars to pay those defense costs was reducing their purchasing power and increasing Healthcare's costs.

Another demand made on the employer's and tax payer's "insurance" dollars during the 1950s and 1960s was the cost of the increasing number of physicians and the cost of the increasing number of specialists.

By the late 1950s and especially during the 1960s, the employer's and tax payer's "insurance" dollars were providing most physicians incomes never considered possible prior to those health insurance programs. For example, most physicians had their offices in their homes prior to the 1950s, but during the 1950s and 1960s, the increasing incomes provided by health insurance was providing physicians the incomes necessary to move their offices out of their homes.

Those increasing incomes were attracting an increasing number of individuals to become physicians, and additional training facilities began to appear for those individuals in "off-shore" medical schools. Also, and the number of foreign trained physicians entering the country was increasing. During the 1960s, and continuing into the 1970s, the physician population was increasing more rapidly than it had increased in the years prior to the 1960s.

Government [Medicare] was foolishly encouraging the increasing number of physicians. The thought was an increasing number of physicians would introduce competition and reduce Healthcare's increasing costs. Wrong. The increasing numbers of physicians increased Healthcare's costs. Next, government froze the provider's reimbursements for their services, but that did not stop the increasing healthcare costs. The increasing numbers of physicians were offering increasing numbers of services to compensate for the frozen service reimbursements.

Was there the need for those increasing numbers of physicians? Or, was their increasing numbers made possible by their costly demands on the employer's and tax payer's "insurance" dollars? Two costly demands were made on the employer's and tax payer's "insurance" dollars during the 1960s that were providing the financial support for the increasing number of physicians. First, patients were using their employer's and tax payer's "insurance" dollars irresponsibly. They were using those dollars to purchase the many medically unnecessary healthcare services their providers were offering. Patients would never have purchased those services when they were using their dollars to purchase their healthcare services. Second, the employers and the government [tax payers] supplying those "insurance" dollars were not monitoring the patient's increasing utilization of unnecessary services, or the provider's increasing charges for those services.

Along with the cost of the increasing number of physicians, there was the cost of the increasing number of specialists. They were demanding and receiving larger "insurance" reimbursements for their services.

Paying the cost of the increasing number of physicians and the increasing cost of the reimbursements for the specialists was requiring employer's and tax payers provide more of their "insurance" dollars. The need for those additional dollars was reducing their purchasing power and increasing Healthcare's costs.

In the 1970s, the costs created by the business entrepreneurs entering healthcare was another costly demand made on the employer's and tax payer's "insurance" dollars. During the 1960s, the billions of "insurance" dollars flowing into healthcare had been attracting business entrepreneurs. They wanted some of those dollars. To enter healthcare, they lobbied Congress to pass the managed healthcare industry legislation in the 1970s. After entering healthcare, those entrepreneurs, along with their investors, created the investor owned and profit driven HMOs and multi hospital management companies.

Those HMOs and hospital management companies have required billions of the employer's and tax payer's "insurance" dollars to fund their management, administrative, and other operating expenses. Also, additional billions of those "insurance" dollars have been required to provide the industry its profits, and to provide the dollars that have made many of the industry's investors millionaires. The need to provide those billions of "insurance" dollars to fund the managed healthcare industry and to provide its profits has reduced the purchasing power of those "insurance" dollars and increased Healthcare's costs.

Only a few of the costly demands made on the employer's and tax payer's "insurance" dollars during the 1950s, 1960s, and into the1970s have been discussed. But the need for those additional "insurance" dollars to pay the cost of those demands reduced their purchasing power and increased Healthcare's costs.

Think about this once again. Prior to the 1960s, one patient dollar was able to purchase one unit of Healthcare's services. But after the 1960s, the need to pay the cost of the many demands made on the employer's and tax payer's "insurance" dollars required many of the employer's and tax payer's "insurance" dollars to purchase the same unit of Healthcare's services only one of the patient's dollar had purchased previously.

Reducing Healthcare's costs requires restoring the purchasing power of the employer's and tax payer's "insurance" dollars. But, how can their purchasing power be restored? Read on.

Chapter Four

Reducing Healthcare's Costs

To paraphrase what someone has said, "Look into the past, and you will frequently find the solution for your problem".

Looking back to 1951 when I began to provide patients their healthcare services, healthcare had neither a cost nor a service availability problem. Both the cost of Healthcare's services and the cost of health insurance were affordable, and the cost of healthcare's services was not increasing. The only demand made on the patient's dollars purchasing Healthcare's services was the need for those dollars to pay the cost of the services patients were receiving. Furthermore, those patients unable to purchase their healthcare services were receiving quality, comprehensive, and easily available healthcare services in the free healthcare facilities.

When we look back at the healthcare delivery system prior to the1960s, everyone had the opportunity to obtain their necessary healthcare services, and Healthcare's costs were affordable. But sixty years later, healthcare has acquired both a cost and a service availability problem. The patient's dollars purchasing healthcare's services were replaced with "insurance" dollars supplied by employer's and tax payer's, and those "insurance" dollars were rampantly being misused by many. Patients were demanding medically unnecessary healthcare services, and becoming indifferent to their increasing cost. In addition to the patient's demands, many costly demands were being made on those "insurance" dollars by the special interest groups entering healthcare[Chapter Three]. Those

19

demands were never made on the patient's dollars when their dollars were purchasing Healthcare's services. The cost of the patient's and the other special interest's demands made on the "insurance" dollars after the 1960s reduced their purchasing power and increased Healthcare's costs. After sixty years of increasing healthcare costs, those costs have become unaffordable and unsustainable.

In addition to Healthcare's increasing costs, sixty years later healthcare has acquired a service availability problem. The closure of the free healthcare facilities in the early 1970s and the failure of Healthcare's providers to provide free healthcare services and their failure to accept insurance reimbursements from Medicare and Medicaid patients has an increasing number of patients experiencing difficulties obtaining their healthcare services.

Is it not obvious! The healthcare delivery system that existed prior to the 1960s had affordable healthcare services and affordable health insurance, and all patients unable to purchase their healthcare services were receiving them in free healthcare facilities [Chapter Eleven]. Everyone had the opportunity to obtain their necessary healthcare services. Also, no costly demands were being made on the patient's dollars purchasing Healthcare's services that would have required more of those dollars to pay those costs.

The historical evidence supports Healthcare's increasing costs after the 1960s were caused by the reduced purchasing power of the employer's and tax payer's "insurance" dollars. The need for more of those "insurance" dollars to pay the cost of the many demands being made on those "insurance" dollars reduced their purchasing power. More of those "insurance" dollars were required after the 1960s to purchase the same unit of Healthcare's services only one patient dollar had purchased prior to the 1960s.

Five changes in the existing private healthcare delivery system are introduced that will reduce the cost of several of those demands made on the employer's and tax payer's "insurance" dollars. Reducing their costs will restore the purchasing power of the "insurance" dollars, and restoring their purchasing power will enable those dollars to purchase additional healthcare services. Purchasing additional healthcare services will reduce Healthcare's costs by at least 40%.

Instead of accepting government's folly of attempting to provide everyone health insurance [Affordable Care Act], the public should consider seriously supporting the five changes proposed in this book. They will provide a private healthcare delivery system with affordable healthcare services and the affordable health insurance Medicare, employers, and other individuals can afford to purchase. Also, the book proposes free healthcare facilities. They will provide those patients unable to purchase their healthcare services better quality, more comprehensive, and more easily available healthcare services than either Medicaid or the Affordable Care Act will provide them [Chapter Eleven].

What are the five changes?

1. Changes in healthcare litigation.
2. Changes in how Healthcare's services are monitored.
3. Changes in how health insurance reimbursements are calculated.
4. Changes in copayment policies.
5. Changes in how hospital insurance reimbursements are calculated.

Before discussing the five changes, a question frequently asked needs to be discussed. Why are so many patients and healthcare providers happy when the cost of Healthcare's services has become unaffordable and unsustainable?

Why are so many patients happy? They have their "free" health insurance, and it has been provided by, and paid for by, someone other than themselves. They have no idea of, and they care less about, how much the cost of their health insurance has increased. Also, patients are happy because their insurance is providing them healthcare services they would never have considered purchasing when they were using their dollars to purchase their healthcare services. Of course, many patients are happy.

But, the probability is the 20% group who require frequent healthcare services will have their happiness become despair within the next decade. Many of their services will be rationed. Also, the probability of the other 80% who require infrequent healthcare services having their happiness become disappointment within the next decade is real. Their infrequently required healthcare services will become increasingly more difficult to obtain and the quality of many of their services will become inferior to the quality they had been receiving.

Unfortunately, the political rhetoric about, and much of the media's reporting of, Healthcare's issues has not prepared the public for what is about to happen to them in the next decade when the Affordable Care Act becomes their healthcare delivery system. Too bad.

If you are a "doubter", ask yourself this question. Is the President and the elected representatives who have supported the Affordable Care Act going to use the Act's services for their future healthcare services? If you believe they are, you must be joking!

Why are Healthcare's providers happy? They have not been challenged when they have increased their service charges or challenged when they have provided patients medically unnecessary services. Both those increasing service charges and unnecessary services are providing Healthcare's providers unprecedented incomes. Furthermore, the profits from their investments in for-profit healthcare facilities are increasing. Of course, providers are happy.

But, the probability of their happiness becoming despair within the next decade is also real. For example, among those providers, there are physicians, and becoming a physicians is rapidly becoming an unattractive career choice for several reasons. One is many of the physicians practicing medicine and surgery are planning to retire as soon as they are able to do so. Many other physicians unable to retire early are planning to limit their patients to those patients with low risk problems. Healthcare litigation will remain a problem for physicians, and with their reimbursements being reduced arbitrarily and significantly, the increasing cost of remaining in practice no longer warrants accepting the risks encountered each day in making medical and surgical decisions.

Those young physicians beginning their practice are creating another reason for our youth to consider becoming a physician to be a bad career choice. Those physicians beginning their practice have acquired large student loans. To quote an alumni appeal for funds to help with student grants, "On average a [the medical school's name] student graduates with over $176,706.00 student loan debt."

The Affordable Care Act's reduced provider reimbursements will not provide these young physicians the income necessary to pay the costs of starting a practice and the cost of repaying their student loans. Also, the uncertainty of what those reimbursements will become has physicians questioning their future incomes. All of these uncertainties are forcing physicians beginning their careers to consider employment opportunities in hospitals and HMOs, or to consider accepting government appointments to positions in rural areas. The need for physicians to retire early, to limit their practices to low risk patients, and to seek employment opportunities is not making becoming a physician appear to be an attractive career choice.

Another reason becoming a physician will be considered a poor career choice is what has happened to their profession's ability to influence their roles in the healthcare delivery system. Healthcare is no longer controlled by physicians. Was the Affordable Care Act conceived and written by practicing physicians? Of course not! Healthcare is now controlled by government bureaucrats, by business entrepreneurs in the managed healthcare industry, and by politically appointed local "community advocate" groups. All three are making Healthcare's decisions, and physicians can do little to challenge those decisions.

There are two reasons physicians are not able to influence their roles in healthcare. One is the medical and osteopathic professions continue their absurd organizational separation and competitiveness. Second, both professions have become splintered organizationally within themselves. Each profession has several different specialties and subspecialties within a specialty, and each specialty and subspecialty has an agenda.

The many different agendas make it impossible for the two professions to muster an effective challenge to anything.

The inability of physicians to influence their future role in the healthcare delivery system makes becoming a physician appear to be a poor career choice.

Sounds bad doesn't it. But, don't worry, if you are older, like me, the probability of what I have discussed regarding patient and provider happiness and future disappointments will not happen to us. What has been discussed will not become apparent until about three years after the Affordable Care Act has become the country's healthcare delivery system—between 2015 and 2017. The probability of my being here in four or more years is not real. But how about you?

Everyone needs to rethink their healthcare priorities NOW, and restoring a healthcare delivery system similar to the one that existed prior to the 1960s needs to be one of their priorities.

If patients and Healthcare's providers were proactive, rather than reactive, which appears to be always the case, and when it is too late, they would be actively supporting the repeal of the Affordable Care Act and replacing it with the five changes and the free healthcare facilities [Chapter Eleven] discussed in this book.

If you are in the 80% group who require infrequent healthcare services, I'm aware of your apathy. BUT what fools you are! You need to become involved in the healthcare debate and rethink your apathy and healthcare priorities. Remember, you too are going to become one of those "seniors" with special healthcare needs and who require frequent healthcare services.

Again, those five changes are:

1. Changes in healthcare litigation.
2. Changes in how Healthcare's services are monitored.
3. Changes in how health insurance reimbursements are calculated.
4. Changes in copayment policies.
5. Changes in how hospital insurance reimbursements are calculated.

Chapter Five

Changes in Healthcare Litigation

Changes in healthcare litigation are the first of the five changes in the private healthcare delivery system to provide a 40% reduction in Healthcare's costs.

Litigation's costs are one of those costly demands made on the employer's and the tax payer's "insurance" dollars, and reducing those costs is necessary to achieve the 40% reduction in healthcare's costs. But reducing those costs will not be easy. Healthcare lawsuits are providing attorneys billions of Healthcare's "insurance" dollars, and attorneys will aggressively challenge any changes that threaten their ability to continue to acquire those "insurance" dollars. Equally difficult will be recruiting some of the public's support for the proposed changes. Many individuals are not aware of, and have had no concerns about, the cost of litigation. Also, they consider litigation to be a lottery. They initiate lawsuits, and they win frequently. Those they have sued settle the lawsuit for a few thousand dollars to avoid a lengthy and expensive legal challenge to their lawsuit.

Attorneys have attempted to protect their interests by stating the proposed changes are not constitutional. They have said individuals with limited incomes would be prevented from initiating lawsuits. Wrong! The proposed changes do not prevent anyone from initiating a lawsuit, or from initiating a lawsuit without any cost to themselves. Instead, the proposed changes only require anyone initiating a lawsuit to question the merits of their lawsuit before initiating their lawsuit. Otherwise, if they were to lose their lawsuit, they would have to pay the defense costs of those they have sued.

Lawsuits were never a healthcare cost problem prior to the 1960s. A healthcare provider's cost of acquiring malpractice insurance was only a few hundred dollars. But after the 1960s, the number of healthcare lawsuits was increasing, and the cost of malpractice insurance increased to its present cost of many thousands of dollars.

By the 1980s, physicians and other providers of Healthcare's services were having to provide a low estimate of 50 billion of their employer's and tax payer's "insurance" dollars each year to pay the cost of defending Healthcare's many lawsuits. Also, many additional "insurance" dollars were required by the 1980s to purchase the medically unnecessary healthcare services healthcare's providers were forced to offer their patients to avoid future lawsuits. Those providers were aware frivolous lawsuits were successful because attorneys were able to convince a jury the provider should have done this or that, rather than what the provider did. Therefore, providers want every possible test, procedure, and study in their patient's record.

Over several decades the cost of having to defend many frivolous lawsuits, and the cost of having to purchase many medically unnecessary healthcare services to avoid future lawsuits have required Healthcare's providers provide billions of their employer's and tax payer's "insurance" dollars to pay those costs. The following two changes in litigation will reduce the need to defend at least 65% to 70% of present malpractice lawsuits, and they will save billions of those "insurance" dollars.

1. Changing financial responsibility—the cost of defense.

The individual initiating a lawsuit has no responsibility for the costs associated with their lawsuit. But, those being sued have the cost of engaging an attorney to defend themselves, and they are unable to recover either their attorney's fees, or the other defense costs, after successfully defending themselves.

A "loser-pays-all" policy is necessary to reduce the number of frivolous lawsuits. The policy makes individuals initiating healthcare lawsuits responsible for the costs created by their lawsuits when their lawsuits are not successful. The need to pay the cost of an unsuccessful lawsuit will have many individuals rethinking the merits of their lawsuit before initiating their lawsuit, and the number of Healthcare's lawsuits would be reduced by at least 60% to 70%. Billions of the employer's and tax payer's "insurance" dollars would be saved.

Furthermore, the loser-pays-all policy eliminates, or reduces significantly, the need for Healthcare's providers to offer their patients medically unnecessary healthcare services to avoid future lawsuits. Eliminating those cost will save additional billions of those "insurance" dollars.

Back in the 1980s I was told by my malpractice insurance company at least 65% of my malpractice insurance premium's costs were paid to the attorneys the insurance company engages to defend physicians in malpractice lawsuits.

2. Changing How Healthcare Lawsuits are Evaluated and Judged.

Both how a healthcare lawsuit is evaluated and how the jurors are selected to judge a lawsuit need to be changed. The proposed changes will save additional employer's and tax payer's "insurance" dollars.

Presently, the evaluation of most healthcare lawsuits is done by an "expert witness" who is paid by the attorneys engaging them. The problem with many "experts" is they functioned more as "hired guns" for the attorneys employing them rather than as "experts" offering testimony a jury member can understand. Also, the "expert's" fees are excessive frequently.

Instead of "experts" being selected by attorneys, the evaluation of a healthcare lawsuit should be done by peers who have no personal or financial interests in the lawsuit. To provide those peers, Medical and Osteopathic Societies should have Medical Malpractice Review Committees. Two peers would be appointed to review a lawsuit. One peer from each of two Societies located in two different communities than the community in which the provider being sued is located. The peers would provide the same service as the service being challenged in the lawsuit.

Providing a peer who performs the same service as the service being challenged in the lawsuit is important, and the failure to provide those individuals has been a problem. Although the "expert" engaged may be a specialists, they may not perform the same specialty's service as the service being challenged in the lawsuit. The best place to find the appropriate specialists is in local Medical and Osteopathic Societies. The peers will be compensated by the insurance company defending the provider according to the Provider Reimbursement Formula. [to be discussed]

In addition to appointing the appropriate peer as the "expert" witness, changing how the jurors are selected in healthcare lawsuits is equally important. An individual is supposed to be judged by a jury of their peers. Selecting the members of a jury from among the general population does not offer a physician, or other healthcare providers, the opportunity to be judged by a jury of their peers.

There are two reasons why the jury selection is important. First is the need to have jurors capable of understanding if there is malpractice [negligence or deviation from accepted standards of care] or mal occurrence. Most Healthcare lawsuits are "maloccurrence" lawsuits. Everything was done properly, but the patient had a bad outcome. Jurors selected from among the general population lack the knowledge necessary to make the appropriate judgment about whether a healthcare lawsuit is maloccurrence or malpractice.

The second reason the jury selection is important is the need to have jurors capable of understanding the medical and surgical issues discussed during a trial rather than having the jury's decision influenced by an attorney.

Attorneys frequently request physicians guilty of malpractice seek a jury trial. Attorneys know juries are sympathetic towards physicians, and an articulate attorney can influence a jury and obtain a favorable not guilty decision when the physician was guilty of malpractice. The attorney's successful not guilty verdict is good for their client, but the not guilty verdict denied a patient the compensation they should have received.

If physicians who perform the same services as those questioned in the lawsuit become the jury members in malpractice trials, patients who have been the victim of malpractice will have a better opportunity to obtain a favorable verdict and receive the compensation they deserve.

Providing physicians the opportunity to be judged by a jury of their peers requires the jurors be at least four physicians. The four would be appointed from each of four Medical or Osteopathic Societies located in four different communities than the community in which the physician being sued is located. Those jurors would perform the same services as the services being questioned in the lawsuit, and they would be appointed by local Medical and Osteopathic Societies. Their compensation would be paid by the court system and additional compensation paid by the insurance company defending the provider. The amount of the compensation would be determined by the Provider Reimbursement Formula.

Many readers are saying, "Are physicians able to objectively evaluate the behavior of other physicians?" Yes, they can, and they have done so very effectively in the past.

Prior to the 1970s, physicians had a credible record of judging the professional behavior of other physicians. For example, I was challenged by my local Medical Society's Ethics Committee around 1960. I was performing a procedure no other physician in the community was performing. I was successful in defending my use of the procedure. But if I had not been successful, I could have been censored. Being censored at the time would have jeopardized my ability to obtain malpractice insurance and hospital privileges. However, today, if I had received the same Society's challenge, I could have avoided the inquiry by threatening a lawsuit against the Society. I'll explain.

The threat of a lawsuit against Medical and Osteopathic Societies by providers whose services were being monitored and challenged created cost problems for those Societies. The Societies had the cost of engaging an attorney to defend the Society, and possibly the cost of engaging an attorney to defend the person monitoring the services. Those legal costs were expensive. Although the probability was both the Society and the person monitoring the services would win the lawsuit, the Society, and the person monitoring, would not be able to recover any of their defense costs after successfully defending themselves. The inability to recover defense costs after a successful defense required Medical and Osteopathic Societies to stop most of, if not all of, their challenges of community healthcare providers.

Adopting the loser-pays-all policy would restore a Society's ability to monitor their community's healthcare provider's behavior and services.

Reducing litigation's costs requires the adoption of the loser-pays-all policy and changing how healthcare lawsuits are evaluated and the jury members are selected. All will reduce the number of malpractice lawsuits significantly and save billions of the employer's and tax payer's "insurance" dollars.

For example, if two peers have identified a lawsuit against a physician to have no merit, the patient would be foolish to initiate their lawsuit. The probability is the four physicians on the jury would agree the lawsuit had no malpractice, and the person initiating the lawsuit would have to pay the defense expenses of the physician they had sued. Likewise, if two peers identified the same lawsuit to have malpractice, the physician would be foolish to request a jury trial seeking a favorable jury decision. The probability is the four physicians on the jury would judge the physician guilty of malpractice, and the physician, not the physician's insurance company, would have to pay the cost of the trial they had requested.

The proposed litigation changes will eliminate the need for healthcare's providers to provide billions of their employer's and tax payer's "insurance" dollars each year to defend frivolous lawsuits. Saving those billions of dollars will contribute to restoring the "insurance" dollar's purchasing power and to reducing Healthcare's costs by at least 40%.

Chapter Six

Monitoring Healthcare's Services

Monitoring Healthcare's services for their medical necessity is the second of the five changes in the private healthcare delivery system to provide a 40% reduction in Healthcare's costs.

When "something" is free—paid by others, there can never be enough of the "something", and neither the need for, nor the cost of, the "something" ever becomes a consideration for those receiving the "something".

In healthcare, the "something" has been the medically unnecessary healthcare service many patients believe themselves "entitled" to receive. Eliminating the insurance reimbursements for those unnecessary services will be difficult. But their elimination is necessary if the 40% reduction in Healthcare's costs is to be obtained.

As has been discussed previously, when the patient's dollars were purchasing Healthcare's services, patients were questioning the need for, and the cost of, the services their dollars were purchasing. But after the employer's and the tax payer's "insurance" dollars began paying for the patient's services, patients were neither questioning the medical necessity of, nor questioning the cost of, the services those "insurance" dollars were purchasing.

As the Medical Director of an HMO, I identified least 30% of the healthcare services offered to our HMO patients as not medically necessary. But many of those services had to be considered "necessary". Physicians were providing those services to avoid future lawsuits. Unfortunately, because of the pressure of frivolous litigation, the HMO's patients continued to receive medically unnecessary services.

Medicare was the first healthcare insurer to initiate monitoring for medical necessity, but Medicare's monitoring had problems. One problem was Medicare employed contractors to perform their monitors. Some of the contractor's denials appeared to be based more on the contractor's wish to impress Medicare than on the medical necessity of the service. Another problem was too many of the individuals employed by the contractors were not qualified to monitor the services they were asked to monitor.

One of my Medical Director responsibilities was to monitor the medical necessity of the services our HMO enrollees were receiving. Based on my observations, there were three reasons why medically unnecessary healthcare services were offered our patients. One reason was too many primary care physicians believed they are exposing themselves to malpractice lawsuits if they did not refer their patients to the more expensive specialists initially. Those primary care physicians had the training to initiated many of the tests and procedures required to evaluate and treat their patient's illnesses. But the threat of a maloccurrence lawsuit prevented them from initiating their patient's initial evaluation and treatment. Those primary care physicians knew a jury selected from among the general population would not be able to understand the difference between maloccurrence and malpractice, and the jury would say the primary care physician was negligent in not referring the patient to a specialist initially.

The second reason medically unnecessary services were offered our patients has been discussed. It was the need for Healthcare's providers to offer their patients medically unnecessary services to avoid future malpractice lawsuits.

The third reason patients were receiving medically unnecessary services was insurance profiteering. Since legal issues have made monitoring for medical necessity potentially expensive for those monitoring the services of others, few healthcare providers wish to expose themselves to a lawsuit that may follow their monitoring and challenging the services of others. Accordingly, healthcare's providers are able to offer medically unnecessary healthcare services unchallenged.

One example of health insurance profiteering appears to be the charge for hearing tests. Prior to the late 1960s, patients receiving hearing tests in most physician's offices and when seeking a hearing aid received their hearing tests without a charge, or in some offices a small charge. But in the late 1950s, or early 1960s, employer's and tax payer's "insurance" dollars began to pay as much as one hundred dollars for the hearing tests, and as much as one hundred and fifty dollars for a hearing aid evaluation. By the mid 1970s, hearing testing and evaluating patients for hearing aids had become a profitable "business" funded by health insurance.

There are two questions that have never been answered with any reliable test retest results. One is are all of the hearing tests an individual receives during a hearing test, and during a hearing aid evaluation necessary? If the insurance reimbursements for hearing tests and for hearing evaluation tests were to stop, how many of those hearing tests now performed would continue to be preformed?

Another example of unnecessary costs are the hearing testing procedures for patients with dizziness. Again, with the limited information obtained from those tests, the probability is some, or all, of those tests would not be performed if insurance was not paying for them.

Another hearing testing issue is why are insurance reimbursements paid to some who evaluate patients for hearing aids and not paid to others who evaluate patients for hearing aids? All are performing the same hearing tests. Also, the same test were administered without any charge prior to insurance paying for them.

Another possible unnecessary cost and suggests insurance profiteering is the cost of the rehab following several surgeries. One example is knee surgery. A patient is sent from the hospital to a nursing home, and for three weeks following the surgery, the patient receives rehab.

When Medicare and the other insurance reimbursements stop, the patient is discharged from the nursing home and the rehab stops. From my observations, most patients could receive their rehab instructions for three or four days in the hospital following their surgery, and sent home to continue the rehab at home. Medicare would not have the cost of three weeks in a nursing home, and the cost of three weeks of rehab. Also, why is both the nursing home and the rehab no longer necessary the day Medicare stops paying for those services?

"Churning", or bring patients back to the office unnecessarily, creates another unnecessary cost. When patients were paying for their office visits, I recall many of my patients asking me if the return visit was necessary. Now patients do not question the need to return to the physician's office. They are not paying for the visit. For example, does every patient have to return to the physician's office to obtain the results of their tests? Or, could the physician's office, as we once did, call the patient about the test's results and have them return to the office when additional consultation and treatment is necessary?

Another example of an unnecessary cost is the elderly who are having difficulty bending over to cut their toe nails. Many go to a Podiatrist office to have their nails cut, and Medicare pays for their nails to be cut. If a person is diabetic, or has problems with their toes and feet, I could understand having a Podiatrist cut their toenails. But is a Podiatrist necessary for others? Also, if insurance was not paying to have the Podiatrist cut the toe nails, many individuals would be having their toe nails cut less expensively in local nail shops.

Another example of medically unnecessary healthcare services are unnecessary surgeries. I recall in the 1960s sardonic comments like, "What is the indication for a tonsillectomy? Blue Cross and Blue Shield", or "What is the indication for a hysterectomy? Blue Cross and Blue Shield." There were others.

There have been, and will continue to be, medically unnecessary procedures and services offered patients as long as insurance continues to pay for them and as long as litigation pressures continue to require them to be offered. Although effective monitoring for medical necessity will eliminate most of those unnecessary procedures and services, effective monitoring will not be possible without the loser-pays-all policy. Those individuals monitoring the healthcare services of others need to be protected from frivolous lawsuits initiated by those whose services they are monitoring and challenging.

An example of a threatened frivolous lawsuit following the monitoring of a physician's services was one I experienced at the HMO. I had questioned the necessity of a service one of our HMO patients had received, and the physician's fee. The physician's response to my inquiry was I would be damaging his professional reputation if I continued with the inquiry, and I had the threat of a lawsuit. The lawsuit would be against me. The probability is I would have won such a lawsuit. But the physician initiating the lawsuit knew I did not want the expense of employing an attorney to defend myself, and he was aware of my inability to recover any of my defense costs when I successfully defended myself. He was correct, and the HMO agreed my challenge of the physician's services and fee would be dropped. How often have the challenges of known unnecessary services had to stop because of threatened lawsuits?

In addition to the loser-pay-all policy providing legal protection for those monitoring the services of others, medical necessity monitor requires qualified individuals to monitor the services of others. The best place to find these qualified individuals is in local Medical and Osteopathic Societies. Those Societies should have Medical Necessity Review Committees, similar to the Committees to review malpractice lawsuits. Those Committees would appoint the appropriate peers to monitor the medical necessity of the services provided by other providers, and they would be compensated by the Provider Reimbursement Formula.

When a provider's service has been identified as medically unnecessary, the provider will have to pay the cost of the monitor. This will discourage providers from offering medically unnecessary services. There would be an appeal process, and two Societies located in different communities would review the previous medical necessity decision.

Although employer's and tax payer's "insurance" dollars will no longer pay for healthcare services identified as having no medical necessity, the patient receiving the services could continue to receive those services if they paid for them.

Since many medically unnecessary healthcare services are being provided patients, there will be many services no longer receiving insurance reimbursements; however, I do not believe patients will have to worry about the future availability of those services. Although they will be available, and patients will continue to want them, the probability of insurance companies offering supplemental insurance programs to pay for many of those services would not be surprising.

At least 30% of present healthcare services will be identified as medically unnecessary and their insurance reimbursements stopped. Many individuals, companies, and organizations will not be happy, and there will be many appeals as well as legal challenges. However, there would be few, if any, legal challenges if the loser-pays-all policy was active.

Saving at least 30% of Healthcare's service costs will save billions of the employer's and tax payer's "insurance" dollars, and those savings will increase the purchasing power of those dollars and contribute to reducing Healthcare's costs by at least 40%.

Chapter Seven

Changing How Health Insurance Reimbursements are Calculated And Awarded

C hanging how health insurance reimbursements to Healthcare's providers are calculated and awarded is the third of the five changes in the private healthcare delivery system to provide at least a 40% reduction in Healthcare's costs.

The reimbursement recommendations in this chapter will not be received either enthusiastically or favorably by many healthcare providers and suppliers. But the recommendations will provide significant reductions in Healthcare's costs, and eliminating those costs will contribute to providing the necessary 40% reduction in Healthcare's costs. Furthermore, the reimbursement recommendations in this chapter offer providers better and more stable reimbursements than the reimbursements arbitrarily established by insurers and government programs.

Insurance reimbursement problems appeared in the late 1950s. The health insurance companies distributing the employer's "insurance" dollars, and later, the tax payer's "insurance" dollars [Medicare and Medicaid] in the 1960s were having problems establishing the amount of money each provider should receive for their services. Initially, the reimbursements were arbitrarily established by the provider. Providers submitted their service charges to an insurance company, and in most instances, the insurance company paid the provider's charges unchallenged. The problem: There were many medically unnecessary healthcare services receiving insurance reimbursements, and there were many disparities in the amounts paid to different healthcare providers. In addition, the increasing charges for Healthcare's services were not being challenged.

The arbitrary process of establishing a provider's insurance reimbursements continued into the 1990s, but instead of the provider, the insurer was arbitrarily establishing the amount of those reimbursements. The problem: The insurers were arbitrarily reducing their reimbursements to Healthcare's providers. Also, the disparities in the payments paid to different providers continued.

Over several decades, establishing the amount of, and eliminating the disparities in, health insurance reimbursements has created the need for a standard to establish those reimbursements. A standard was proposed in the late 1980s, but it received no attention. The standard was labeled a price control, and at the time, price controls were considered inappropriate because they had not been successful in the free market economy.

But as has been discussed previously, healthcare is not part of the free market economy, and price controls have a place in healthcare. In free market economies, consumers have the opportunity to decide if they wish to purchase a product, or a service, and they have the opportunity to determine the price they are willing to pay to obtain the product or service. However, in healthcare, patients have neither the option of deciding if they wanted to acquire their illness or disability nor the option of deciding how much they will pay to treat their illness or disability. Accordingly, price controls have a place in controlling the cost of Healthcare's services, but establishing the "price" cannot be an arbitrary process. A standard is necessary to establish that "price" [reimbursement].

A standard [price control] was proposed in the late 1980s. It was the Provider Reimbursement Formula, and the Formula had then, and continues to have, three components. They are:

1. The cost of the provider.

    The Formula assigns an hourly payment rate for all of healthcare's providers. This is not new among professions.

2. The time required to complete a service.

    The Formula assigns a time for the completion of all of healthcare's services—office visits, procedures, laboratory studies, X-rays, rehab services, etc. With few exceptions, the time required to complete all of Healthcare's services is established and easily obtained. The Formula refers to the time required to complete a service as the "service time".

    Each year a physician has 46 weeks to accumulate their "service time" [Six weeks for vacation and meeting times] If the physician provides patients services for 40 hrs. /week for 46 weeks, the physician has accumulated 1840hrs. of "service time" during the year.

3. The office overhead allowance.

    In addition to the insurance reimbursement for a provider's "service time", the Formula provides an additional reimbursement for the provider's office overhead expenses. Since different healthcare specialties and services have different office requirements, the reimbursements for the office overhead allowance will not be the same for all specialties and services. But each will have a specified amount of money allowed for its annual office expenses. Also, the amount of the office overhead allowance awarded to each physician in a group practice using the same office, or several offices, will vary.

To calculate the amount of an office overhead allowance, every office is considered to be open to provide patients their services 40 hrs./week for 52 weeks/year, or a provider's "office availability time" is 2080 hours annually. Their office overhead items are:

1. The cost of, the number of, and the type of, office personnel required to provide the specialty's services.
2. The specialty's office space requirements.
3. The cost of, and the depreciation allowance for, the equipment required to support the specialty.
4. The specialty's disposable items.
5. Utilities, and other office maintenance expenses.
6. There may be others.

If the physician or other healthcare provider wishes to have more space, personnel, etc. than the Formula allows, they may do whatever they wish. But the Formula pays for only what it allows.

When I think about the need for providers to receive insurance reimbursements for their office expenses, I think of my grandfather and my uncle. Both were physicians, and both, like most physicians prior to the 1950s had their offices in their homes. Health insurance had not become the primary source of payment for Healthcare's services, and the cost of operating an office was an expense requiring frugality.

The following example is the calculation of the Office Overhead Allowance for a physician practicing as an independent practitioner in specialty A.

a. The specialty's required office personnel are a secretary, a receptionist, and a nurse.
b. The specialty's office space requirement is 5,000 square feet.
c. The cost of the specialty's equipment depreciation is?
d. The average cost each month for the specialty's disposals is?
e. The average cost of utilities each month is?
f. The average office maintenance costs for office square footage allowance each month is?

The following is an example of how the Formula calculates the insurance reimbursement for this physician.

1. The cost of the provider.

    The hourly rate for a physician is $200/ hour [negotiable].

2. The time to complete the service.

    This physician has provided patients enough healthcare services during the year to have accumulated 1500 hrs. of "service time" of the possible 1840 hours of available "service times" [40hrs./week X 46 weeks/year], and the physician's insurance reimbursement for the 1500 hrs. of "service time" was $300,000 [$200/ hr. X 1500 hrs.].

3. The Office Overhead Allowance.

    The office overhead allowance is based on the provider's "service time", and every provider's annual "office availability time" is 2080 hrs. [40hrs./ week X 52 weeks].

In this example, the Formula has allowed this physician's specialty an annual office expense of $150,000. Therefore, each hour of this physician's "service time" receives an office overhead allowance of $74 [2080 hours of "office availability time" divided into the allowed $150,000 for the office expenses].

The annual insurance reimbursement for this physician's Office Overhead Allowance is $111,000 [1500 hrs. of "service time" X $74]. The physician's "service time" was 1500 hrs. during the year, and for each hour of "service time", the physician received $74 for their office overhear expenses.

The annual total insurance reimbursement for this physician is $411,000. [$300,000 for "service time", and $111,000 for Office Overhead Allowance].

The following is an example of the Formula's calculation of the insurance reimbursement for a specific surgical procedure whose present insurance code number is WXYZ, and whose present surgeon's fee is $3,000.

1. The cost of the provider:

   The provider is a physician who receives $200/hr. of "service time".

2. The time required to complete the operation.

   a. Time to complete the pre-op. records: * * * * 15 min.
   b. Time to complete the surgery * * * * * * * 3 hours
   c. Two daily post-op hospital visits for six days @15min./day
      = 1 1/2 hrs
   d. Time to complete the post-op, records*****15 min.

   The total "service time" for this surgical procedure is 5 hrs. and the reimbursement for 5 hrs. of "service time" is $1,000. [$200/hr. X 5 hrs. = $1,000]. Every physician performing this procedure whose insurance code number is WXYZ receives $1,000.

3. The Office Overhead Allowance.

   The office overhead allowance for this physician's specialty is $67 for each hour of the physician's "service time". The physician's Office Overhead Allowance is $335. [$67 X 5 hrs. = $335]

   The physician's total insurance reimbursement for this surgical procedure is $1,335. The Formula has saved $1,665.

What benefits does the Formula offer?

1. The Formula provides the standard necessary to establish the amount an insurer pays a healthcare provider for all healthcare services—for office visits, procedures, X-rays, laboratory studies,etc. and,

2. The Formula eliminates the provider's and the insurer's arbitrary calculation of those insurance reimbursements.

3. The Formula eliminates the disparities in the amounts paid to different physicians.

It takes the same amount of time, knowledge, training, and skill be become a Board Certified physician who provides no procedure services [primary care physicians] as it does to become a Board Certified physician who provides procedure services [surgeons]. Therefore, larger insurance reimbursements for procedure services cannot be justified.

4. Eliminating the payment disparities will save billions of health insurance dollars, and will,

5. Encourage more graduating medical and osteopathic students to become primary care physicians rather than becoming one of the physicians who receives the larger insurance reimbursements for their services.

To obtain the equal reimbursements for their services, future primary care physician will have to be "Board Certified". Obtaining the Certification requires completing a four year residency training program after graduating from their Medical or Osteopathic schools followed by passing the "Board's" examination for their specialty. Primary care physicians are family physicians, internists, and pediatricians.

Only one example of how the Formula calculates an insurance reimbursement has been described [a surgical procedure], but the Formula calculates the reimbursements for office visits, laboratory studies, X rays, etc. the same way. For example, the Formula recognizes only three "service times" for office visits—a five minute office visit, a fifteen minute office visit, and a thirty minute office visit.

Computers have made the application of "service times" for reimbursements possible, and providers requesting unusual "service time" reimbursements can be easily identified.

The Formula will save billions of the employer's and tax payer's "insurance" dollars each year, and contribute to providing the 40% reduction in Healthcare's costs.

Chapter Eight

Changes in Copayment Policies

Co-payments are the fourth of the five changes in the existing private healthcare delivery system to provide at least a 40% reduction in Healthcare's costs.

There is a direct relationship between patients having to pay for their healthcare services and the cost of those services. Again, prior to the 1960s, when patients were using their dollars to pay for their healthcare services, they accepted only medically necessary healthcare services and questioned their costs. But after the 1960s, employers and tax payers began to pay for their services, and patients began to utilize more services, and they were no longer questioning either the medical necessity of, or the charges for, their services. Since most patients will continue to have insurance paying for their healthcare services, the need to have patients share in the cost of their services is necessary.

However, copayments do have a down side. Co-payments are an expense, and not infrequently, those patients with special needs requiring frequent and expensive healthcare services have denied themselves necessary healthcare services because of their need to pay a copayment. Copayments for these patients will have to be either modified, or eliminated.

Although some patients will object to having to contribute towards the cost of their services [copayments], they need to understand how copayments benefit them. When the utilization of healthcare's services increases, so does the cost of both the patient's taxes and the products and services the patient purchase. When employers have to provide more of their dollars to pay the increasing cost of their employee's health insurance benefits, the employer recovers those costs by increasing the price of their products and services. Also, when the government has to provide more tax dollars to pay for Medicare's and Medicaid's increasing costs, government increases the public's taxes to recover those costs. Accordingly, patients benefit when they utilize fewer healthcare services.

A suggestion for establishing the amount of a copayment is to have the amount become a percentage of the Formula's insurance reimbursement for the service. For example the copayment for the first $1,000 would be 10%. A $100 service charge would have a copayment of $10. For each $500 after the initial $1,000,the copayment would be 5%. A $1,500 fee would have a copayment of $100 for the $1,000 plus a $25 for the $500.

Chapter Nine

Changes In How Hospital Insurance Payments are Calculated

Changing how insurance payments are awarded to hospitals is the fifth of the five changes in the private healthcare delivery system to provide at least a 40% reduction in Healthcare's costs.

Prior to the 1970s, the hospital system was a not-for-profit and charitable system offering free hospital services in many state, city, county, and local hospitals, and everyone had the opportunity to receive their necessary hospital services. Those individuals with the means to pay for their services either reached into their pockets for the cash, or they used the hospital insurance they had purchased, to pay for their hospital services. Those individuals without the means to pay for their hospital services received them in the hospital's outpatient clinics and inpatient hospital wards without a charge for their services.

During the 1950s and 1960s, increasing numbers of patients were acquiring hospital insurance and hospitals were becoming profitable. By the 1970s, those profits had attracted business entrepreneurs who wanted some of those profits. But they had no way of entering healthcare until Congress passed the manage healthcare legislation in the 1970s. The legislation offered those entrepreneurs their opportunity to enter healthcare, and after entering healthcare, they attracted investors. Together with their investors, entrepreneurs established the investor owned and profit driven multi-hospital management industry. The industry began to acquire the not-for-profit hospital system, and within a decade, the previously charitable and not-for-profit hospital system had become an investor owned for profit driven multi-hospital business system.

As the hospital system was becoming a profit driven business system, the cost of hospital services was increasing, and hospitals were no longer offering free services. Without the free services, patients unable to pay for their hospital services and patients with inadequate hospital insurance were having difficulty obtaining those services.

Profiting from a patient's need for a hospitalization is unacceptable, and like Healthcare's providers [The Provider Reimbursement Formula], hospitals need to have price controls applied to the cost of their services. Price controls can be applied by regulating the services, and the cost of the services, a hospital is allowed to apply to each hospitalized patient's daily charges for its fixed costs, and by monitoring the medical necessity of the hospital's variable costs.

FIXED COSTS

A hospital's fixed costs are always present regardless of the number of patients in the hospital, and many of those fixed costs can be either reduced or eliminated. Some are:

1. Hospital construction costs.

A new hospital I visited recently had the majority of its beds in private rooms. My immediate response was the cost of so many private rooms was architecturally unnecessary and fiscally irresponsible. The construction costs of the walls necessary to make single bed hospital rooms and the long corridors to service those rooms is very expensive, and single rooms are not medically necessary.

Back in the 1960s, while participating on a Committee to construct an addition to the hospital, I encountered the beginning of the influence hospital insurance was to have in creating increasing hospital costs. An increasing number of patients entering the hospital had hospital insurance, paid by someone other than themselves, and their insurance was beginning to change their thoughts about many of their hospital services. For example, "privacy" and "conveniences" were to become frequent requests, and since insurance was making hospitals profitable, hospital management was acquiring a business mindset of its need to accommodate those patient requests—soon to become demands. To paraphrase my question to the Committee, "Are we to assume the hospital system is becoming a competitive business system like hotels? Because if hospitals were going to become like hotels, the cost of hospitalization would be increasing, and those costs would be medically unnecessary costs." But I lost. Two and single bedrooms were constructed to provide patients their privacy and conveniences.

Unfortunately, during the 1960s, both patients and hospital management were becoming indifferent to increasing hospital costs. Why should they have concerns? Unregulated hospital insurance was paying those costs.

Like so many "modern" hospital administrators, and their "insurance carrying" patients, the lack of "privacy" and "conveniency" requests prior to patients acquiring hospital insurance paid by someone other than themselves was being forgotten. Prior to insurance, patients had been satisfied with the four or six bedrooms when they were paying for their hospitalization, and patients unable to pay for their hospitalization were satisfied with rooms with ten or more beds. Private rooms were rare, and existed primarily for patients requiring isolation.

A fact: The walls necessary to create one and two bed rooms and the long corridors necessary to serve those rooms have created unnecessary and expensive hospital construction costs. Another expensive and unnecessary hospital construction cost is the aesthetics incorporated into many hospital building programs. Those aesthetics may appeal to patients, but they create medically unnecessary hospital fixed costs. Are hospitals to become competitive based on their conveniences and aesthetics or on their ability to treat patients?

Hospital insurance can no longer afford to pay for the privacy, for the conveniences, and for the aesthetics the public with their insurance paid by someone other than themselves is demanding. Hospitals are not luxury hotels. The public needs to rethink their hospital priorities and focus more on what is medically necessary for their hospital to provide them to restore their health.

There are other hospital construction costs that are medically unnecessary fixed costs. They need to be reviewed and their costs either reduced or eliminated.

2. Specialty hospitals.

Hospitals offering only one specialty's services were common prior to the 1970s, and the hospital system needs to return to one hospital in large communities providing one of the more expensive specialty's services in addition to their other services. Providing the same service in several hospitals in the same community increases the cost of providing the service in each hospital.

3. The cost of the investor owned for-profit driven multi-hospital management companies.

Using a patient's need for hospitalization to provide investors and entrepreneurs' profits is not an acceptable hospital fixed cost. Examine for yourself the management and investor costs of the multihospital management industry. You may be surprised how much their costs have increased the cost of your hospitalization and the cost of the insurance your employer or Medicare has been providing you.

Too many with whom I have discussed the issue, do not understand the economics of healthcare. Few understand why a community's hospital providing medical and surgical services should not be a profit generating business while a local business providing a product or service should be encouraged to make a profit. Both are employers, and both are needed in every community. But hospitals and businesses are different economically.

Starting a business requires taking a risk, and the business, and its investors, hope the community's consumers will purchase, and will pay the price the business is asking for, its product and service. However, the business is aware the community's consumers do not have to purchase their product or service. But, if the consumers purchase, and pay the asking price for, the product or service, the business is successful and makes a profit. Also, the business can continue to employ people and possibly employ more people. If however, the consumers do not purchase the product or the service, the business goes out-of-business, and its investors lose their money. Also, the employees lose their jobs.

In contrast, starting a hospital does not require taking a risk. All of the community's consumers are going to require the hospital's services at some time in their lives. Also, when they acquire their need for the hospital's services, they will not have the option of deciding whether or not they want to enter the hospital. They must enter the hospital, and they must pay the hospital's charges. This is why profiting from a patient's need for hospital services is both unacceptable and unconscionable.

I'm aware someone will know of a hospital that has closed. But an examination of that hospital will probably show it was a hospital started during the 1960s or 1970s when hospitals became profitable, and hospitals, like hotels, became competitive businesses rather than hospitals a community required to accommodate its healthcare needs.

Another very expensive and unnecessary cost consuming many "insurance" dollars is the medically unnecessary positions the investor owned and profit driven hospital systems are creating. Since both local and federal governments have become major players in the hospital system, hospitals are creating positions for the purpose of obtaining "political favors". The excessive salaries and benefits paid those occupying those positions must no longer be allowed as a hospital's fixed cost.

Furthermore, having served on hospital Boards, the not-for-profit hospital system never paid their Board members. Therefore, when the investor owned and profit driven multi hospital management companies pay their Board members, those costs should not be allowed as a hospital's fixed cost.

4. Hospital regulations.

Most hospital regulations are not medically necessary. Most have been created to sustain the many unnecessary healthcare bureaucracies created following government entering healthcare in the late 1960s. Hospital regulations need to be reviewed, and most of them eliminated. Their costs create unnecessary fixed costs.

5. Hospital litigation.

Lawsuits are a significant hospital fixed cost, and adopting the "loser-pays-all" policy would reduce those costs significantly.

6. Hospital education programs.

Hospital education programs were never funded when hospitals were not-for-profit, and funding those programs now with hospital "insurance" money is neither necessary nor acceptable. Those costs are an unnecessary fixed cost.

7. Hospital marketing programs.

The expensive marketing of a hospital and its services with radio, TV, print, and other media advertising should not be allowed as a hospital's fixed cost. Those marketing programs began in the 1970s after Medicare initiated monitoring for medical necessity. Many Medicare hospital admissions were denied. I can remember patients entering the hospital for their annual physical examinations.

The number of patients in hospitals dropped significantly following Medicare's medical necessity monitoring, and many hospital beds were empty. To fill those beds, hospitals started marketing programs to attract patients.

There are other fixed costs that need to be reviewed and either reduced or eliminated from a patient's daily hospital charges.

VARIABLE COSTS

Variable costs are those cost created when hospital services are provided patients, and those costs will vary with the number of patients in the hospital and with the cost of the services provided those patients.

Controlling a hospital's variable costs requires recording all of the services each hospitalized patient receives during their hospitalization and the cost of those services. Accounting systems are available, and they have been used, to record those costs. One accounting system is the DRGs [Diagnostic Related Groups]

When Medicare was established, hospitals could not tell Medicare the cost of treating different illnesses. To establish those costs, Medicare had Yale University's Public Health Dept. develop the DRGs [Diagnostic Related Groups]. The DRGs placed the many different illnesses into groups. Each patient admitted to the hospital had their illness assigned to one of those groups, and all of the services the patient received, and the cost of those services, were recorded in the patient's record.

Using information from accounting systems such as the DRGs, hospitals can identify the cost of treating different illnesses; can identify the cost of treating each patient's illness; can identify the cost of treating different patients with the same illness; can identify the cost of treating the same illness in different hospitals in the same community or region; and can identify the medical necessity of the services each Medical Staff member provides their patients. Accounting systems such as the DRGs are needed to control a hospital's variable costs. At each monthly department's Medical Staff meeting, the physicians, and other hospital departments, need to review their department's DRGs and other variable costs.

Penalties are necessary for Medical Staff members who provide medically unnecessary services, and the DRGs can identify those physicians. One penalty is a "bed tax". Each day a patient is hospitalized, the physician admitting the patient is charged a "bedtax". When the patient is discharged, if the cost of the services the physician has provided their patient is equal too, or less than, the average DRG cost of treating the same illness in the region's other hospitals, the physician does not have to pay the "bed tax" for that patient. Of course there are medical reasons why a DRG may be more expensive than the region's DRG, and the opportunity to appeal the more expensive DRG would exist.

At this time, a "bed tax" would be a problem. Medical Staff members have litigation pressures, and they are providing their patients medically unnecessary services to avoid future malpractice lawsuits. Adopting the "loser-pays-all" policy would eliminate, or significantly reduce, a physician's need to provide their patients unnecessary services to avoid future lawsuits.

Reducing or eliminating many of a hospital's fixed and variable costs would reduce hospital costs significantly, and billions of the employer's and tax payer's "insurance" dollars would be saved. Those savings would contribute to achieving the 40% reduction in Healthcare's costs.

Chapter Ten

The Challengers and
The Five Changes

The five changes proposed in the previous chapters can anticipate encountering many challengers. The five changes threaten the power and the profits of many individuals and organizations. If the five changes replace the Affordable Care Act, politicians will lose their opportunity to control healthcare, and their opportunity to obtain the enormous political power control would have provided them. The business entrepreneurs and their investors in the managed healthcare industry will aggressively challenge the five changes. The five changes introduce price controls, and those price controls will reduce the industry's ability to generate profits. Without profits, there would be no investors, and the survival of the managed healthcare industry would be questionable. Some of Healthcare's suppliers will challenge the five changes. They will reduce their ability to engage in health insurance profiteering. Defense attorneys will challenge the five changes. They will cost their profession billions of dollars. Patients receiving medically unnecessary healthcare services will challenge the five changes. Medical necessity monitoring will have many of their services become ineligible to receive health insurance reimbursements. Physicians, and other healthcare providers, will challenge the five changes. The Provider Reimbursement Formula will reduce many of their insurance reimbursements—but the Formula will increase the reimbursements for primary care physicians. Also, the profits many physicians, and the other healthcare providers are obtaining from their investments in for-profit healthcare facilities will be either reduced or eliminated. Need I go on?

Although the five changes will have many challengers, those patients who are informed, and who are aware of the benefits the five changes would offer them will become proactive. They will become the challengers of the challengers. If you question why you should become one of those challenging the challengers, step back for a moment and separate yourself from the political rhetoric and misinformation. Think about why Congress has passed legislation creating the Affordable Care Act but does not want the Act to become the delivery system until after the 2012election.

If you recall what was discussed previously, the Affordable Care Act is a political document. It is not a healthcare document. The Act was conceived to create more tax revenue to support a bigger government, and to create a large voting block dependent on government for their healthcare services. The public's dependency would provide politicians enormous political power. Since the Act cannot, and it was not conceived to, benefit either the public or improve the healthcare delivery system, neither Congress nor the President want the Act to become the delivery system until after the 2012 elections. Read the Act and you will agree with me, and you will become one of those challenging the challengers of the five changes.

The goal of the public's challenge needs to be replacing the Affordable Care Act with a healthcare delivery system similar to the one that had existed prior to the 1960s. It was a delivery system offering everyone the same opportunity to obtain quality, comprehensive, and easily available healthcare services from the healthcare providers of their choice and from healthcare providers who have come from the best of our youth. The proposed five changes and the free healthcare facilities [discussed in the next chapter] provide the delivery system that existed prior to the 1960s.

Also, if you question your need to become a challenger, ponder this. Within the decade following the Affordable Care Act becoming our country's healthcare delivery system, the probability of both a physicians shortage, and those training to become physicians not coming from the best of our youth is real. When the public becomes aware of both the physician shortage and the service quality issues becoming problems, those issues will become greater problems when the public awakens to the fact they will have to live with those shortage and quality issues for at least another ten to twelve years. Why?

Once the public become aware the delivery system has not provided the career opportunities necessary to attract the best of our youth to become the delivery system's physicians, the public's demands to change the system will take probably two years for government to make the changes, and will probably take another two years of marketing the changes to have the best of our youth graduating from colleges consider becoming a physician to be a good carer choice once again. After entering Medical and Osteopathic schools, those students will require at least another eight years to become well trained physicians [four years in medical or osteopathic schools and at least four years in a residency training program].

Don't doubt me! If I'm fortunate and live until 2015, I will be witnessing what I just described. Doesn't prevention make more sense than allowing the demise [death] of our healthcare delivery system go unchallenged. Without the public's challenge, the avarice [greed] of a few, and the lust for power by another few will create a delivery system unlike the delivery system that existed prior to the 1960s.

Support the five changes!

What about those free healthcare facilities discussed so frequently in the text?

They are up next.

Chapter Eleven

The Free Healthcare Facilities

History has provided the evidence. The utopia some seek in which everyone is provided health insurance is neither practical, realistic, nor fiscally responsible. Health insurance has been used irresponsibly by many over the past sixty years; has increased Healthcare's costs unnecessarily; and has not provided everyone the same opportunity to obtain their necessary healthcare services.

Medicaid is an example of health insurance not offering EVERYONE the SAME opportunity to obtain quality, comprehensive, and easily available healthcare services. Most of our country's healthcare providers do not want to provide Medicaid patients their services, or accept their low insurance reimbursements. Consequently, many Medicaid patients, as well as those patients unable to pay for their services, have difficulty obtaining their services.

Instead of Medicaid, this book recommends replacing Medicaid with state sponsored free healthcare facilities. Those facilities will provide ALL patients unable to purchase their healthcare services the opportunity to obtain the same quality, comprehensive, and the easily available healthcare services as the services provided patients who pay for their healthcare services.

Unfortunately, in 2011 discussing the subject of free healthcare facilities creates an unfavorable "knee-jerk" reaction from most patients and from their healthcare providers. Their problem is both are too young to have experienced the benefits offered by a healthcare delivery system offering free healthcare services. I'll take a moment to discuss my experiences, and why I know from those experiences, patients will benefit more from the free healthcare facilities proposed in this book than they will from Medicaid or from the Medicaid proposed in the Affordable Care Act.

In 1951, I began providing patients their healthcare services in free healthcare facilities located in state, county, city and local community hospitals, and for about twenty years thereafter, I continued to provide patients their healthcare services in those free facilities while teaching students and resident physicians their medicine and surgery. My experiences were always favorable. Patients in those free facilities received services that were of better quality, more comprehensive, and more easily available than the services most Medicaid patients have received, and the services all patients without Medicaid and the ability to pay for their services have received.

There are stories about bad outcomes in the free healthcare facilities, but most of those stories are hearsay. From my observations, those stories come from individuals who are too young to have witnessed any of the bad outcomes they claim occurred.

Yes, I have witnessed bad outcomes, but those bad outcomes did not occur until the late 1960s. Medicare and Medicaid had been introduced, and both were providing many patients who had been receiving their services in the free healthcare facilities health insurance. Fewer patients were participating in the free facilities. Also, an increasing number of physicians were no longer volunteering their services in those free facilities. Those physicians were leaving the free facilities to treat an increasing number of patients with health insurance in their offices. As fewer patients were attending the free clinics, and as fewer physicians were available to treat those patients, I witnessed some bad outcomes in the free facilities.

But, from the 1950s through the late 1960s, there were many patients receiving their healthcare service in the free facilities, and there were many physicians volunteering their time to treat those patients. During those years, I do not recall witnessing any bad outcomes in the large free healthcare facilities in which I participated. Also, those patients received better services less expensively than the services most Medicaid patients have received.

Those free facilities need to be restored, and this book proposes each state replace its Medicaid program with free healthcare facilities. Each state's Dept. of Health will assist each county's, or city's, Dept. of Health to establish its free healthcare facility, or facilities. The state will fund the free facilities, and there are several models of how the free facilities should be structured. One is the V.A. medical system.

The free facilities will provide outpatient services in existing local hospitals, and in other buildings in the community. Although those community hospitals may be investor owned, the economic impact of the five changes on the healthcare delivery system will have many of the investor owned hospitals welcoming the opportunity to lease some of their space for their community's free outpatient clinics.

When free facility patients are hospitalized, their services will be provided in multi-bed rooms. The free facilities will lease space in existing hospitals and will remodel the space for their patients to occupy. Most free facilities will employ a hospitalist, and the other personnel, to staff and provide the facility's hospitalized patients their services. A hospitalist is an employed physician who spends all of their time in the hospital providing patients their services, or monitoring the services consulting physicians are providing their patients. In smaller communities, the free facility's primary care physicians may choose to have local hospital personnel provide the free patients their hospital services. The Provider Reimbursement Formula, or other contract arrangements, will establish the reimbursement policies for those providers.

Each patient will be assigned to a free facility, and they will receive an identification card. On the card will be the name of the free facility they have been assigned, and the name of the primary care physician they have been assigned. The patient's primary care physician will be responsible for, and will monitor, all of the patient's healthcare services. Appointments will be necessary with their physician.

Some of the free facilities will be open 24 hours seven days a week to offer emergency services. Or, in smaller communities, the hospital's emergency room may be a better choice to provide the night time and weekend services.

The cost of each patient's services, regardless of where obtained, will be recorded [DRGs] and paid by the free outpatient facility the patient has been assigned. The Provider Reimbursement Formula, or other compensation contracts, will establish the reimbursements for services provided by providers not employed by the free facilities. Transportation issues will vary in different locations. Ambulance services will be monitored for medical necessity.

Every free healthcare facility will benefit by the adoption of the loser-pays-all policy and the Provider Reimbursement Formula. Why? Each facility's primary care physician is responsible for their assigned patient's services. The loser-pays-all policy will enable those physicians to feel more comfortable providing their patients the many services they are capable of providing those patients rather than having to refer the patient immediately to one, or more, of the various specialist outside of the free facility. Those referrals are an expense for the free facility. At this time, the threat of a lawsuit has primary care physicians referring patients to specialists immediately. The problem is even after a primary care physician has provided their patients the appropriate services, patients have initiated malpractice lawsuits, and they have frequently won those lawsuits. A jury selected from among the general public does not possess the medical knowledge necessary to understand the difference between maloccurrence [everything was done properly] and malpractice. Accordingly, juries have offered guilty verdicts when they were mislead by an attorney into believing the doctor should have referred the patient immediately to a specialist.

In addition to the cost benefits offered by the loser-pays-all policy, an additional benefit provided by the adoption of the five changes is the Provider Reimbursement Formula. The Formula provides primary care physicians the same compensation for their services as all other physicians receive for their services. Accordingly, instead of physicians graduating from Medical and Osteopathic schools becoming the specialists who receive the larger insurance reimbursements, many of those graduating students will be attracted to becoming the primary care physicians required by the free facilities.

Few, if any, specialists will be employed by the free facilities. Their services will be acquired by referrals from the facility's primary care physicians or from the facility's hospitalist. The specialist's reimbursements will be established by the Provider Reimbursement Formula, or by other contract arrangement, and will be paid by the free outpatient facility the patient has been assigned.

Nurses and other appropriate personnel will be employed by the free facilities. However, many of the free facility's nursing services can be provided by nursing students supervised by the graduate nurses employed by the free facility. This was the practice prior to the free facilities closing in the 1970s.

There are other free facility services individuals can provide without compensation. People receiving welfare payments, or people completing community service obligations, can provide those services. Working in the free facilities would offer those individuals the opportunity to learn skills that would offer them the opportunity to find future employment.

Unfortunately, physicians can no longer be expected to provide their services without compensation in the free healthcare facilities as they did prior to the free clinics closing in the early 1970s.

Prior to the 1970s and the introduction of the investor owned multi hospital management industry, hospitals were not-for-profit and charitable. Also, each hospital's Medical Staff member was obligated to provide their services without compensation in their hospital's free outpatient clinics and inpatient hospital wards. Why? Physicians were able to admit their patients to their not-for-profit hospital and use the hospital's resources to treat their patients without any cost to themselves. In return for their admitting privileges, and for the use of the hospital's resources, the hospital's physicians were expected to provide their services without compensation to their hospital's free patients during designated times. But there is no probability of this happening.

States will find funding their free healthcare facilities to be less expensive than funding Medicaid had been, and they will find those facilities are providing services to more patients unable to pay for their services. Furthermore, the bureaucracy required in each state to administer the state's free healthcare facilities will be much smaller, more effective, more efficient, and less expensive than the bureaucracies required by the federal government in Washington, D.C. to administer Medicaid's and the Affordable Care Act's Medicaid services in all fifty states.

Another advantage of the proposed state funded free facilities is local philanthropy. It will play a role in each community's free healthcare facilities, as it did prior to the 1970s. Philanthropists are more willing to support local activities than they are national activities.

Another important reason why free healthcare facilities are better than Medicaid is each patient in a free facility has an assigned primary care physician monitoring the appropriateness and necessity of their services. In contrast, each Medicaid patient has no one monitoring the appropriateness and necessity of their services.

Primary care physician is a generic term. Those physicians are Internists, Family Practitioners, and Pediatricians. Acquiring those primary care physicians [The Provider Reimbursement Formula],and providing them protection from frivolous maloccurrence lawsuits [loser-pays-all] requires the five changes.

A potentially serious problem free healthcare facility must anticipate encountering is the Medical and Osteopathic schools competing for the free facility's patients. Both schools need a patient resource for their training programs. The closure of the free healthcare facilities in the early 1970s created a patient resource problem for all schools training physicians. The free facility's patients had been the patient resource for teaching students their clinical sciences—how to diagnosis and treat patients. To replace the patients in the free facilities, private patients were used, and many private patients did not want students examining and participating in their treatment program. Therefore, both schools are in need of a patient resource for training their students, and both will be competing for the free facility's patients.

The free facilities must establish the rule that each free facility's primary care physicians and the facility's hospitalists will control the treatment programs provided the free facility's patients. Otherwise, the misuse of those patients could become a serious problem.

Why the need to anticipate the competition between the two schools requires some discussion. Let's begin by stating there is no longer any difference between a graduating D.O. [osteopathic] physicians and a graduating M.D. physician. However, there will always be a physician and a physician's physician. The physician's physician is the physician other physicians use for themselves because that physician has better skills. My internist had been a D.O. Also, there is no reason for the continued existence of separate schools to train D.O. and M.D. physicians. The continued separation of those schools is fiscally irresponsible. But when you look into the past, you can understand the reason for the ridiculous and continued separation of, and competition among, M.D. and D.O. physicians.

Prior to World War II, osteopathic [D.O.] physicians had their own training facilities and hospitals, and the military did not recognize D.O. physicians. The D.O. physicians were not drafted, and as the M.D. physicians entered the military, the D.O. physicians became the country's primary care physicians. After World War II, the D.O. physician wanted the same recognition as the M.D. physician. They have obtained that recognition.

During the 1950s, another controversial professional issue surfaced. Many M.D. physicians were beginning to specialize, but the D.O. physicians did not have the specialty training opportunities. The specialty programs training M.D. physicians and the specialty "Boards" examining and certifying those physicians did not recognize D.O. physicians. Accordingly, most D.O. physicians remained Family Physicians. However, during the 1960s, the much larger insurance reimbursements being offered specialists created income issues. More D.O. physicians wanted to become those "Board Certified" specialists and receive the larger insurance reimbursements.

During the 1960s, D.O. physicians were receiving appointments in the M.D. specialty training programs, and those D.O. physicians became specialists with the same training as the M.D. specialist.

Those D.O. specialists either became members of M.D. hospital Medical Staffs or they returned to their D.O. hospitals and developed specialty training programs in those hospitals.

Unfortunately, those M.D. and D.O. physicians who received their training before the 1980s have continued the professional competitiveness, and they have encouraged the professional separation of the two professions. An example of how ridiculous their competitiveness had become was establishing a four year school in the 1980s to train only D.O. physicians in a community in New Jersey that had an existing much less expensive school teaching M.D. students their clinical sciences [how to diagnosis and treat patients] during their last two years of medical education.

At the time, those challenging the need for the proposed D.O. school received much criticism form both M.D. and D.O. physicians. Paraphrasing some of the comments of those opposing the new D.O. school, there was no need to fund an expensive and unnecessary four year school graduating only D.O. physicians. This comment received criticism from the D.O. physicians who wanted the separate school. Another comment was there was no longer any difference between D.O. and M.D. physician. This comment received criticism from some M.D. physicians. Another comment was since there is no longer any difference between D.O. and M.D, physicians, there should be only one education program [school] training future physicians. The students graduating from those schools could choose either a D.O. degree or a M.D. degree. This received criticism from both the D.O. and M.D. physicians.

Unfortunately, the state legislature funded the more expensive and unnecessary four year osteopathic school training only D.O. physicians in the same area as the M.D. training school.

To be both professionally proactive and fiscally responsible, the M.D. and D.O. professions need to become one profession as the allopathic [medical] and homeopathic professions became around the 1900s.

Returning to the discussion of free healthcare facilities, this book maintains healthcare is a right. The right implies everyone must be offered the same opportunity to receive the same quality, comprehensive, and easily available healthcare services. Adopting the five changes and the free facilities, instead of attempting to offer everyone health insurance, is the best way to provide everyone that right. The five changes will provide the affordable health insurance Medicare, employers, and many individuals can afford to purchase. Those patients would enjoy the privileges their health insurance provides. They would have the opportunity to obtain their healthcare services in a fee-for-service private healthcare delivery system in which they have the option of selecting the providers of their choice and from providers who have come from the best of our youth.

For those individuals without either health insurance or the ability to pay for their healthcare services, this book maintains those individuals have the right to obtain the same quality, comprehensive, and available healthcare services as the services provided those patients who are paying for their services. To provide those individuals those services, state sponsored free healthcare facilities will be available.

When I think of all my friends with Medicare seeking their healthcare services in the V.A. hospital system, there may be a need for the proposed free facilities to offer two services. One service would be to restrict the free facility's free services to patients unable to purchase their healthcare services, and the patient's eligibility to receive those free services would be based on their income. Another service would be to provide the opportunity for patients with health insurance to pay for a free facility's services.

Past history has provided the evidence. Restoring free healthcare facilities similar to free facilities that existed prior to the 1960s is the best way to provide EVERYONE the opportunity to obtain their healthcare services. While the five changes are providing the affordable health insurance Medicare, employers, and many individuals can afford to purchase and can be used to obtain their healthcare services, the free healthcare facilities are available to provide ALL patients unable to purchase their healthcare services their opportunity to obtain the same quality, comprehensive, and available healthcare services as the services patients with health insurance are receiving.

After providing patient's their medial and surgical services for almost forty years, and after providing patients their services in the free healthcare facilities for twenty of those forty years, I know more patients without the ability to pay for their healthcare services were able to receive better quality, more comprehensive, and more easily available healthcare services less expensively in the free healthcare facilities than patients without the ability to purchase their services have received from Medicaid or can anticipate receiving from the Affordable Care Act's expanded Medicaid program.

If the future healthcare delivery system is to benefit patients, restoration of the proposed state sponsored free healthcare facilities along with the five changes need to be the public's healthcare priorities.

Chapter Twelve

What is Ahead?

What's ahead? Ahead is a combination of increasingly complex treatment programs and a declining mortality rate. Both will be challenging the healthcare delivery system's ability to provide, and to fund, those increasingly complex treatment programs to an increasing population of seniors who create at least 80% of Healthcare's costs.

The public should be questioning, based on the history of other existing government programs, the ability of the Affordable Care Act to provide those increasingly complex treatment programs to an increasing population of seniors. Isn't it obvious the five changes and the free healthcare facilities would be better choices.

The probability is the Affordable Care Act will have difficulty attracting the best of our youth to become the providers required to provide those increasingly complex services; the probability is the Act will have difficulty making the changes in the delivery system required to accommodate those increasingly complex healthcare services; and the probability is the Act will have difficulty funding those increasingly complex treatment programs to an increasing number of seniors without significant increases in taxes and rationing.

Instead of blindly accepting the Affordable Care Act with its many inadequacies, the public should be rethinking their need for government to provide them their healthcare services. Instead, the public should be considering alternative healthcare delivery systems like the one proposed in this book. This book has proposed fixing Medicare, replacing Medicaid, and repealing the Affordable Care Act as the best way to provide EVERYONE the same opportunity to obtain their medically necessary healthcare services. Fixing Medicare will provide the affordable health insurance, and replacing Medicaid with the free healthcare facilities will offer ALL patients unable to purchase their healthcare services the opportunity the obtain same quality, comprehensiveness, and availability healthcare services as the services provided patients purchasing their services.

But, let's deal with what we have. We have two problems. First, too many individuals in the United States have acquired a debilitating dependency on, and obsession with, health insurance. Second, many of those individuals appear to have accepted the folly government has proposed that everyone needs to have health insurance in order to obtain their healthcare services. An example of this is a community in the New York area electing a person to Congress because the person said they would not touch Medicare.

Was the electorate foolish, irresponsible, and dysfunctional? Foolish, perhaps. But irresponsible and dysfunctional? No! Their voting represents how poorly informed the electorate is in the United States about healthcare issues. Politician's with their self serving rhetoric and a complying media have been able to create unwarranted fears among voters. Every election has some politicians saying, "Don't allow such and such [a political candidate] take away your Social Security or your Medicare". Yet, every politician knows both Social Security and Medicare will never be abandoned, and the proposals to make both viable into the future will not change any of the necessary benefits offered those now receiving Social Security and Medicare—or change any of the benefits those anticipating receiving Social Security and Medicare in the next decade or more.

Wake up America!

If voters want to have fears about their future healthcare services, they better wake up and become aware of the problems they will have obtaining their healthcare services when the Affordable Care Act replaces Medicare and Medicaid and becomes the healthcare delivery system in the United States.

Also, those voters need to have concerns about the probability of the Affordable Care Act's "insurance" being worthless within a decade. The Act has not offered the career incentives necessary to attract the best of our youth to become our future physicians, and without physicians to provide Healthcare's services, health insurance is worthless.

An immediate problem for all voters is engaging the 80% of the population in the United States who require infrequent healthcare services in the healthcare debate before it is too late. As of now, the 80% group will regret not having been engaged in the healthcare debate when the Affordable Care Act becomes their healthcare delivery system. I can hear those individuals in 2015 or 2016 saying, "What happened?" "Why is it so difficult to obtain my services?" "What do you mean my mother is too old to have a knee replacement?

One final comment for those voters in the New York area, and everyone else. You need to begin thinking positively about unnecessary healthcare services becoming increasingly difficult to obtain regardless of the delivery system offering those services. It should be obvious to you by now, the five changes and the free facilities offer you the best opportunity to continue to receive ALL of your necessary healthcare services. Also, remember, the medically necessary services the five changes and the free healthcare facilities will be offering you are the same services you would have been purchasing prior to the 1960s when your dollars were purchasing only medically necessary services. Now, however, you are more fortunate. The insurance someone else has provided you is providing you the same medically necessary services "free".

But don't panic! Those services you enjoyed receiving that were not medically necessary will continue to be available for YOU to purchase with your dollars. Or, supplemental insurance programs will be available you can purchase to pay for many of those services that are not medically necessary. Those supplemental insurance programs will probably be like the present Medicare prescription program. A list of services will be available along with the price of the insurance to purchase those services.

At my age, I have no interest in the job, but let's say I have the job of obtaining support for the repeal of the Affordable Care Act and its replacement with the five changes to fix Medicare and the free healthcare facilities. What would I be doing?

First, I would probably be very frustrated. I'm struggling to obtain the support of the 80% of our population who require infrequent healthcare services. Their support is needed to have a strong lobby to move our elected representatives in Congress to repeal the Affordable Care Act. In addition, I'm having difficulty instilling into their minds the importance of the five changes and the free facilities. Unfortunately, many individuals within the group remain apathetic.

Second, I'm making many powerful individuals and organization very angry with me. Many members in Congress are angry, and I can hear both those Congresspersons seeking a National Health Service and their supporting members in the media attempting to defame and discredit me. If you cannot attack the message, you attack the messenger. This will not be a new experience for me. I'm 85, and I have had several controversial responsibilities. Also, I'm aware I've made mistakes—haven't we all? But, so what! Bringing those mistakes to the surface may be refreshing. I'll see if I have learned from them. Damage me? I'm retired, and how many more years am I going to be around? Not many. So, bring it on . . . .

A variety of other individuals and organizations are angry. They were discussed in Chapter Ten. But here is a quick review. The loser-pays-all policy has made many attorneys angry. Monitoring the medical necessity of Healthcare's services has many individuals angry. The Provider Reimbursement Formula has many healthcare providers and suppliers angry. Copayments have some individuals angry. The business entrepreneurs and their investors in the managed healthcare industry are furious. Recording the cost of the services a hospital's Medical Staff member provides their patients and comparing those costs with other physician's services [DRGs] has some Medical Staff members angry.

Need I go on listing those angry with me?

Yes many are angry with me. But, what about the 80% who require only infrequent healthcare services. Have they learned anything from the anger of so many for what I'm doing? The anger should provide them evidence of how irresponsibly patients, Healthcare's providers and suppliers, and many other special interests have used health insurance, and how their misuse of health insurance has created a plethora of medically unnecessary healthcare services and costs. Also, they should be aware of how government has used health insurance to obtain the political power they seek by their controlling healthcare.

But, has all the anger thrust at me given the 80% cause to rethink their need to support me? Apparently not. Some of their services have been denied insurance reimbursements, and the medical necessity of their services makes no difference to most of them. They believe they were entitled to receive those medically unnecessary services.

Let's see if the next discussion of the probability of what I believe lays ahead three years after the five changes and the free healthcare facilities have been adopted attracts the attention of the 80%group and provides me their support. I believe it will.

The time frame is three years later. The Affordable Care Act has been repealed, and the five changes have been adopted. It took about six months using the existing insurance code numbers to establish the Provider Reimbursement Formula's "service time" reimbursements for Healthcare's many services. Medical and Osteopathic Societies have established Medical Malpractice Review Committees and Medical Necessity Review Committees, and more and more healthcare services are being judged medically not necessary by those Committees. The loser-pays-all policy has been adopted, but the jury selection process continues to be discussed. Copayments have been established for all of Healthcare's services, and copayments have the local public "advocacy" groups demanding their elected representatives in each state make the hospital licensing laws force every hospital to publish their fixed and variable costs for public review and possible action. Also, price controls have the multi hospital management companies and HMOs having solvency problems. The goal of a 40% reduction in Healthcare's costs is about to be reached.

Medicaid has been replaced with state sponsored free healthcare facilities, and the adoption of the five changes has the Provider Reimbursement Formula providing the free facilities attractive compensation packages for their primary care physicians, and the loser-pays-all policy is providing the incentive for the free facilities Internists, Family Physicians, and Pediatricians to initate their patient's initial treatment programs. Also, the approaching 40% reduction in Healthcare's costs is making free facilities solvent, and the states are pleased with how inexpensive the free facilities are to operate when compared with their previous Medicaid costs.

Health insurance is affordable, and government [Medicare], employers, and other individuals are purchasing the insurance. Medicare has been preserved and continues to provide all of their medically necessary services. In addition, increasing numbers of employers are purchasing the affordable health insurance, as are many individuals.

Everyone is being provided the SAME opportunity to obtain their necessary healthcare services and the services are less expensive. Also, the patient and provider friendly private healthcare delivery system has been preserved, and patients with their insurance have the opportunity to select the providers of their choice. Furthermore, becoming a physician continues to be a desirable career choice

A healthcare delivery system similar to the one existing prior to the 1960s has been restored. But what kind of a healthcare delivery system is it? Also, has it attracted the support of the 80%?

The affordable health insurance is being sold by many different PRIVATE insurance companies, and each company is offering their insurance in as many states as each company wishes to participate. The health insurance sections of the insurance companies are not-for-profit or the amounts of their profits are regulated. There is a competitive bidding process among these private not-for-profit insurers, and both Congress and employer's are purchasing the insurance. What the insurance policies are offering is regulated by each state's insurance regulations and is subject to medical necessity monitoring.

Although Medical Necessity Committees have many healthcare services no longer receiving insurance reimbursements, the same insurance companies are offering supplemental insurance program to provide payment for many of those medically unnecessary services.

A savings program has been incorporated in those affordable health insurance programs. The savings programs are optional, and the money is invested by the insurance company so that young policyholders will have the opportunity to accumulate the money necessary to purchase the services they might want to obtain later in life when Medicare is not providing those services.

The five changes are changing the delivery system. Up until recently, the delivery system was not accepting the concept of multidisciplinary treatment centers for treating complex illnesses like cancer. But because of the economic impact of the Provider Reimbursement Formula, the economic impact of monitoring healthcare's services for their medical necessity, and the economic impact of the increasing complexity of Healthcare's services and treatment programs physicians are leaving their solo and group specialty practices and forming multi-specialty group practices—a group of physicians each with a different specialty and subspecialty. Those groups are structured like the existing Mayo, Cleveland, and other multi-specialty groups. Also, since the Provider Reimbursement Formula's compensation relief and the loser-pays-all policy's litigation relief, primary care physicians are forming group practices in increasing numbers and they are providing annual "treatment packages" to provide a patient their primary care services for a year.

In addition to multi specialty physician groups and primary care physician groups changing the delivery system, the increasing complexity of Healthcare's services and treatment programs is changing how the health insurance industry pays for Healthcare's services. For example, seniors with their frequent illnesses, and variety of their illnesses, require the more complex treatment programs, and their numbers continue to increase each year.

Those complex treatment programs require the services of several physicians, and the need for an insurance company to pay each of those physicians separately for their services, and to pay each of those physician every time they provide their services has made the fee-for-service reimbursement process become cumbersome and expensive for patients requiring those prolonged and complex treatment programs. Instead of the fee-for-service payment process, the insurance companies are providing "treatment packages" for those illnesses requiring the complex treatment programs. The reimbursements for all of the numerous services these patients will require during the active treatment of their illness [not for the semiannual or annual check-ups following the active treatment] are included in the "treatment package". In addition to the "treatment packages" for patients requiring the more complex treatment programs, other patients are purchasing similar "treatment packages" for themselves to pay primary care physician groups for their services for a year. All of those costs are payable with the Provider Reimbursement Formula's reimbursements—price controls.

States are contracting with the multi specialty physician groups and providing them similar "treatment packages" for the free facility's patients with chronic illnesses requiring the complex treatment programs. Contracting with those groups insures the free facility's patients receive quality and comprehensive treatment programs, and the states have found the "treatment packages" to be less expensive.

It all sounds good, but there is nothing to stop Healthcare's providers from independently increasing their service charges to compensate for the Provider Reimbursement Formula's price controls. Or, is there something to stop them? The probability is few, if any, Healthcare providers will increase their patient charges for several reasons. One reason is they are able to recognize that fixing Medicare with the five changes and replacing Medicaid with the free healthcare facilities creates a fee-for-service private healthcare delivery system that is best for them in the future. Also, the providers recognize the Provider Reimbursement Formula's reimbursements offer better reimbursement opportunities than the bureaucratically and arbitrarily established reimbursements offered by the Affordable Care Act. Furthermore, since patients are contributing to the cost of their services with their copayments, they will be seeking other providers who have not increased their charges. Those patients will have other options available to them they do not have now. I can envision those free facilities, along with the multi specialty physician groups, and primary care physician groups offering "treatment packages" that accept the Provider Reimbursement Formula's price controls. The primary care groups will be providing "treatment packages" to provide the day by day infrequently required healthcare services families require, and the multi specialty groups will be offering "treatment packages" for the treatment of the chronic illnesses requiring prolonged and more complex treatment programs.

The probability of the five changes and the free healthcare facilities being our healthcare delivery system and creating the delivery system described above after three years is real. But the probability of this delivery system becoming reality is dependent on the support of the 80% of the public who require infrequent healthcare services. Without their support for the repeal of the Affordable Care Act and its replacement with the five changes and the free facilities, the Act will be our country's future healthcare delivery system.

Again, the question the public needs to ask themselves is will the President and his family and the Congresspersons who voted for the Affordable Care Act and their families be using the services offered by the Affordable Care Act? Now they have very special insurance programs, and believing they will drop those programs and accept the services of the Affordable Care Act is capricious thinking. However, if the President and those Congresspersons who voted for the Affordable Care Act were interested in the public's healthcare needs and not in the political power they will lose, they would repeal the Affordable Care Act and replace it with the five changes and the free healthcare facilities.

Is the pain of restoring fiscal sanity to our healthcare delivery system going to create a biblical healthcare Armageddon among the 80% who require infrequent healthcare services? Or, will that 80% be able to recognize that fixing Medicare with the five changes and replacing Medicaid with the free healthcare facilities will created a healthcare delivery system that will be best for them in the future. If those 80% look beyond the present, they will realize they are going to become older and become a member of the 20% group requiring frequent and expensive healthcare services. At that time, the best opportunity for them to receive their necessary healthcare services is with a fixed Medicare [the five changes] and free healthcare facilities. Otherwise, the 80% need to prepare themselves to be able to purchase their own healthcare services from a select group of providers privately, or to prepare for rationed healthcare services during their senior years.